# FALLING

# FOR A

# DOLPHIN

also by Heathcote Williams
Whale Nation

# HEATHCOTE WILLIAMS

# FALLING

# FOR A

# DOLPHIN

HARMONY BOOKS / NEW YORK

Published in 1989 in the United States of America by Harmony Books, a division of Crown Publishers, Inc., 225 Park Avenue South, New York, New York 10003

Originally published in 1988 in Great Britain by Jonathan Cape Ltd.

HARMONY and colophon are trademarks of Crown Publishers, Inc.

Printed in the U.S.A.

Book design by Jennifer Harper

Library of Congress Cataloging-in-Publication Data
Williams, Heathcote.
Falling for a dolphin.
1. Dolphins—Poetry.  I. Title.
PR6073I4278F35   1989      821'.914      88-34707
ISBN 0-517-57299-0
10  9  8  7  6  5  4  3  2  1

First American Edition

It is an important and popular fact these things are not always what they seem. For instance, on the planet Earth, man had always assumed that he was more intelligent than dolphins because he had achieved so much—the wheel, New York, wars and so on—whilst all the dolphins had ever done was muck about in the water having a good time. But conversely, the dolphins had always believed that they were far more intelligent than man—for precisely the same reasons.

Douglas Adams, *The Hitchhiker's Guide to the Galaxy*

# FALLING FOR A DOLPHIN

"Is there anything else you need . . . ?"

A wet-suit lies on the diving-shop floor:
An undulating mass of black and red blubber.
Beside it, a bag of industrial polythene,
Filled with breathing-tubes, weights, and weight-belt;
Palm-shaped flippers, and a mask.

"No," says the proprietor,
"Just add water. To taste."

Daingean Uí Chús.
The Eask Peninsula.
At the edge of the Atlantic.
Dawn.
Outcrops of metamorphic rock,
Formed two hundred million years ago,
Crumpled sheets, and rippling curtains of mud,
Slowly tilted upright, and petrified,

Great gray escarpments, tipped with blanket bog.

The turf-topped ruins of beehive houses,
From the Stone Age,
Dot the landscape, like blunt canines.

Disused cornfields crumble into the sea . . .
Clumps of thrift.
Only the faintest ghosts of tillage.

Round ziggurats of stone
Washed down by the tides
Into splintered spirals,
Like Towers of Babel,
And layered with seams of illusory Kerry diamonds.

Sheer slabs of steel-blue stone,
Sixty feet high,
Cracked by the sun,
Loom out of the sea.

A set built a hundred and seventy million years
Before the birth of the Himalayas;
Inaccessible from land.

The caves, made from collapsed leaves of *millefeuille*
    rock,
Echo with the conversation of guillemots,
Wheatears, choughs, and gannets.
Sea-crows, large as umbrellas,
Take an unhurried view of any outside visit.

A water-hen pecks silently for mussels.
Foam hisses through cracks in a reef.

The only mammal for miles is rumoured to live here.
A hermit dolphin.
Quietly fishing for pollock, wrasse, and conger;
Occasionally diverted by fishermen:
Riding their bow-waves,
Treating their boats as ambulatory Jacuzzi,
Racing and overtaking ninety-horsepower engines;
Then shooting towards the pale blue mountains
Of Macgillycuddy's Reeks . . .
Vanishing in search of some more testing sport.

The lighthouse keeper, Paddy Ferriter,
Sighted it four years ago;
Then a local fisherman, Lawrence Benison,
Passed on the changing details of its solitary haunts.

This I-Spy genealogy led to an invitation:
"You must come."

A week later, the wet-suit,
Inhabited,
Lies spread-eagled on the surface of the water.

Mauve jellyfish drift past,
Blinking their whole bodies.
Like them, you move only with the wind and the tide,
Nature's public transport.
The individual will is put on hold.

Fronds of kelp and dulse, strapped to the bottom,
Surge and thrash below you,
Caught in submarine storms
That feature in no weather report.

You waft in random directions:
First towards the Inch, then Crow Rock,
Then Doulus Head, and then the Blasket Islands.

You flick your fingers noiselessly underwater,
As instructed.
You tap the metal weights upon your belt
Repeatedly with a pebble
Clutched in the cold fingers of one hand.

There is no sign of it.

You remind yourself that the creature,
Somewhere in this chilling expanse of water,
Is wild, and not a dog, or a cottage cat
To be manipulated.

It can detect you from five miles distant,
Make up its own mind whether or not to appear . . .
And there may be more of its mind to be made up.

There is still no sign of it.

Adrift in the sea,
In a mild state of sensory deprivation,
Your inner voice becomes more audible:
Demanding to know, from time to time,
What on earth it is that you think you are doing.

You swim a few masterful strokes, in response;
While being blown about, uncontrollably,
As directionless as a piece of litter.

The Atlantic currents have quickly taken you
Half a mile from shore.
The inner voice persists.
You reply to it by thinking that you are no longer quite
    on the earth,
Where that inner voice has hatched its authority,
But now suspended between one world and another.
A world where you have no bearings,
Like a hang-glider lost in umapped continents of clouds.

Voices from the night before
Now make themselves heard with added impact:
Warnings of compass-point jellyfish
With thin, spidery tentacles,
Inducing coma, then drowning . . .
Lethal as curare;
Porbeagle sharks, brought in by a warm spell,
Surface swimmers, nine feet long . . . .

The pebble takes on more significance:
Your grip on this acoustic distress-flare tightens,
It is pathetically tapped with greater frequency.
To no effect.
The Atlantic rollers flick at you,
Like school bullies
Remorselessly tormenting some hapless victim with wet
    towels,
And reminding you that death lives very locally,
About six inches away.

Then you remember the last voice of the night before:
". . . Just call its name."
"Its name . . . ?"
"It has a load of names . . . ."
He shrugged.
"We just call it the dolphin.
You call out 'Dolphin' and it comes."

You call, repeatedly;
Shouting the word into the salty gusts of wind sweeping
    into your face,
Then absurdly diving beneath the surface to escape a
    driving shower;
To see again if there is any sign of it below.

There is none.

Slowly you forget about it,
And forget the dangers, so teasingly described,
As you drift across the surface,
Half-hypnotised.

A scrap of your old, reptile brain
Freshly reminds you
That you came from the sea;
That you are composed mainly of water . . .
And so, being here,
Unwillingly bent double,
Mauled by Atlantic swells
Upended by the undertow
Is not wholly incongruous.

A fleck of flesh,
Coated in rubber;
Once on land,
Now back in the water;
And peering down at a translucent underworld
In an atavistic trance.

As lumpy tussocks of water smash together
You are ionised by the charge,
Contact-drunk on the sea.
Every drop of it descended
From cometary ice.

The water,
To which you owe your life,
First came to the planet
As a rain of icy comets,
Which then dissolved,
Vaporising on impact with the earth's aurora.

. . . You peer down
At minute ancestors,
Moving with ease through three dimensions
As if still in the space they came from.

You gaze at the delicate life forms that begat you:
Developing just beneath the surface
To seal themselves off from harmful ultraviolet light.

You float along the ceiling of another kingdom,
Looking down, into the vague regions of your past.

Silica dust quivers, constantly,
Shimmering through the water
Like the clouds of multicoloured phosphenes
That gather together within your closed eyelids
Before you fall asleep.

Suddenly, your blood undergoes a sea-change.
Your body jerks, shuddering like a rocket on takeoff—
Half in the air, half still in ground-effect—
The rumoured creature lies beside you in the water.

A bare hint of movement in its tail,
Then quite still.

Eye to eye.

Twelve, fifteen foot long.
Half a ton in weight.
Sleek, and silvery as the moon.

It has approached you, indetectably, from behind.
You suppress an impulse to spin round hastily:
Anxious to see from where, exactly, this apparition
    came,
Fearing you would take in water through the tube,
And drown.

It draws closer,
Setting no wash.
Staring.
Its gray, telling eye
Inches from yours.

You stare back, startled,
Caught off guard by an intelligence
Both knowing and remote.

With a single movement
It disappears;
As if to allow you to digest the visitation.

When the involuntary spurts of adrenaline
Discharged into the surrounding water
Are diluted,
And the shock-waves have ebbed,
It returns.
To move up and down your body,
Spraying each section of it with a barrage of echo-
    locating clicks:
Penetrating your brain, heart, lungs, stomach, groin,
    legs and feet
Seeming to gauge each in depth . . .
Mapping your body's geography
In punctilious detail.

Your brain tingles oddly,
As it is spattered, in a second examination,
With unfathomable waves of sound and ultrasound.

The dolphin then rises to the surface
Releasing a deep gust of air from the top of its domed
    head;
And inhales beside you.

The valve in its blowhole closes—
A faint chink of cartilage . . .
The unexpected sound of breathing,
In isolation, in the ocean,
Creating an arresting affinity.

Two air-breathing mammals, side by side:
One blinkered, uncoordinated
And cluttered with plastic accessories;
The other in careless control,
A wide-eyed virtuoso,
Master of a larger territory than yours
And, unlike other animals,
Unnervingly disinclined to be outstared.

Your skin prickles,
Physically registering its prodigious strength;
Quickening you to the fact that one dissembling move,
The betrayal even of one false thought you're prone to
   feel . . .
And it could stave in your body
With a lackadaisical flick of its fin.
Torpedo into you at thirty knots,
Snapping your spine as if it were a sardine's,
Crush each limb into fragments with its jaws,
And eighty-eight needle-sharp, conical teeth.

But it appears to entertain no such wish.
And all such apprehensions are swiftly dissolved
By its expression:
A three-foot smile,
A tender-lipped antidote to panic.

Its face is permanently engraved with this subtle,
    potent smile,
As if a smile were the only facial gesture worth making,
And it had therefore settled into a genetic trait:
The emblem of its seductive ability
To disarm a fellow-creature—
Whom history could have persuaded it
Was its most intractable enemy—
By the only safe method: making friends.

Close to,
The benign fixture becomes more complex:
The smile flickers from a droll interest, through
    bemused pity
To a wry, patrician glance of transcendence.

The dolphin's presence in the water,
Electrically alive to each goggle-eyed gaze,
Each hampered, blundering movement in the water,
Poultices out embarrassed gurgles, by way of greeting.

Despite yourself, you are compelled to speak:
To blurt out a succession of stilted, staccato phrases
    through the breathing-tube . . .
". . . Hello,"
And, "I'm pleased to meet you . . . ."

Each one more prostratedly foolish than the last.
And each one barely intelligible,
Even to your own ears,
Spluttered through water,
Its little sense buried by burbling gasps.

The dolphin whistles, then clicks, rhythmically,
Then makes a sound like the creaking of a door,
A rusty hinge; it whistles again.
There's a rattle, resembling a chuckle.

You try to guess the meaning from its tone,
Like a tongue-tied foreigner,
Desperately striving to understand the hermetic kernel
    of a language—
The sure clue to consciousness.

It speaks again.
You make some spontaneous noises in reply,
Less inhibited.

The dolphin draws closer,
Gently nudging your mask with its upper lip,
To expose your face.

It touches you.
Your inner workings conducted through its jaw.
It touches your cheek,
Nuzzling your skin,
Then moves away
With a glance that seems to invite you
To stroll, horizontally, in a direction of its choosing.

You accept.
Magnetically allured by a very complete stranger.
Willingly locked into its company.

You tentatively reach out
To stroke its smooth, unscaled skin,
Soft as a child's flesh,
As you waft silently in the dolphin's company
Past the Foze Rock, the Tailor's Iron,
The Sorrowful Cliffs,
And a reef called the Bank of the Gardens of the Mouth.

Marooned beside a living raft,
And understanding how sea-creatures of the past
Were reputed to beguile sailors:
Persuading them that they were entering a well of
    forgetfulness—
Unaware that in the sharp bliss of that sea-creature's
    song
Centuries were passing.

The distant landmass loses its pull.
You swim together,
Enmeshed in a febrile elation;
Running away to sea.

Your lungs, two portable sacs of air—
Eight pints, now treasured instead of being taken for
    granted—
Are spun out, like emergency rations
As you descend
To greet it below.

It disappears, in a puff of spray,
Then reappears so quickly on the horizon
You think it must have a companion . . .

It plunges, lost to view.

You wait.
Lost now without it.
Five minutes . . . ten . . .
Vulnerable. A little afraid.

A dark fin surfaces, fifty yards away . . .
Your inner voice, still auditioning,
Whispers "Shark,"
It has been whispering the word constantly
As you peered at every fin-shaped wave,
Relieved when the tense tip spilt and broke.

The dark fin approaches,
The frisson, induced by the uncertain silhouette,
Serving to remind you of the received wisdom of your
    tribe—
On the off-chance you had been tempted
To hurl it overboard.

The dark fin draws closer still.
Your reason tells you that the sharks here
Are filter-feeders, harmless, even a threatened species,
There'd be a million-to-one chance against meeting a
    blue shark,
An occasional summer migrant.
But your reason is unceremoniously drowned in sweat.

The dark fin is beside you.
. . . The dolphin's fin,
Shaped like a thorn on a rose.

It finds its way to you
With the accuracy of a bat
Beaming in on a moth.

An hour goes by.
Side by side with someone as strange
As a mixture of a Martian and a mermaid,
In alien territory.

Its rounded, orb-like head
Containing a brain
The size of yours,
And half as big again.

An intelligence nurtured in the sea.
One that has arisen quite unassisted
By the surfeit of stimuli
The human intelligence has concocted
To gorge itself upon.

Its foetal features
Compelling you to wonder with what plot
Evolution may decide to favour it.

There's a distant splash.
You look up, and see a long, mottled fish,
Flashing and spinning vertically above the water,
Its scales coruscating in the sun, like mica.

It's being hurled up vigorously from below,
Fifteen, twenty feet,
Then it falls, smacking the surface;
Three times,
Then silence.

You scrutinize the ripples,
And vainly scan the surface of the water.

Then your hand is brushed insistently from below
By the tail of a black pollock
Held in the dolphin's mouth.

You lower your head into the water.
It is presented to you.
Its flesh unblemished, drowned by air.
Vitamin-fresh sushi.

Stunned, you attempt a token bite,
And then return it, to be swallowed in one clean suck.

You stare at each other;
The sense of some old alliance, rekindled;
And you brood upon the truth of the old wives' tale
Of fish being good for the brain:
The lipids and protein in fish
Now revealed to have a similar structure to cerebral
    tissue—
And fish is a diet you both have in common.

It vanishes again, inexplicably,
Through the jade-green mist,
To digest the pollock . . . ? to sleep . . . ?
To fish again . . . to drift in thought . . . ?
Then, like lightning, reappears
Uncannily choosing moments
When you are thinking of it
The most intently.

And you become easily, euphorically persuaded
By this large, eerie, and susceptive presence
That you are exchanging particles of thought.
Mutually mixing some telepathic cocktail.
You know, instinctively, that there is some strange
    exchange,
And you become quite unconcerned
By the thought of shore-based familiars
Snorting with derision at the soft-headed crankiness
    of it,
For without this indefinable exchange
You would be drawing a blank,
Cutting the dolphin dead.

And your mind feels recharged by the nameless
    wildness of this creature,
So stretched that you effortlessly think of it as a person,
Of your two minds blending,
Your mind reaching out and becoming one with another.

And if bioelectricity travels beyond the cranium,
As it does,
And if a current travels faster through water,
With less resistance,
As it does,
Then who knows that a dolphin doesn't overhear what
    you're thinking.
When its elevated head lies in the water next to yours,
It's not hard to think that it does.

A mosaic of sound-waves,
Compressed, then rarefied, then compressed again,
Penetrates your mind.
First what seems like a mimicry:
Of your own burbling in the water,
Then a stream of imitations
Sounding like trains, planes, car-horns,
Noises picked up from the shore, your habitat,
And relayed back to you,
Now estranged,
As if by way of reassurance.

The dolphin then reverts to its own language,
Flooding you with a barrage of pulsed tones.
The sounds have a disturbing effect
As if there were some huge bird impossibly flying
    underwater beside you,
Singing.

You feel for a moment as if you have wandered into
    some subterranean cavern
Decorated with an arcane script,
And you can only continue in an obscure rite of passage
By deciphering it . . .


You are compelled to reply,
Without knowing what your reply is in response to.
And as you become caught up in this one-way
    conversation,
Out of your depth,
And as the high-frequency sounds pervade you,
They seem to be slyly skinning you of antique
    armouring,
Stressful inconsistencies.
Your grip on the little basket of human manias you
    clutch so firmly
Relaxes . . .
You begin to think how little there is to prevent you
    staying . . .
The cold . . . ?
Now overcome by this large, warm drop of flesh beside
    you.

The rush of abstract sound ebbs . . .
Was it just some signal,
A series of conditioned signals
Invisibly designed to stun a prey . . . ?
Even if it was only that,
It has succeeded.

The dolphin stares at you.

When scientists scan the universe for intelligent life
Preference is given to those planets which are water-
base.
The dolphin's elusive sapience prompts unaccustomed
questions:
Who is to say that *you* are in sole charge of
evolution . . . ?
That you are the be-all and end-all
Of this particular planet's experiment in self-
awareness . . . ?
Only you.

The refreshing tribal treachery
Rousing thoughts of what might have been
Had your genes been pointing in another direction . . .
That the past, differently handled,
Could have been the springboard
For a quite different present.

For what explains the curious sense of being greeted by
    the dolphin
As a long-lost friend . . . ?

Was it that once upon a time,
You both grew up together?
The cave-dwelling human, living off crustaceans,
Anxious to form some compact with the dolphin,
A superior hunter whose skills you admired . . . ?
The dolphin, in its turn, intrigued by the dexterity of the
    human hand . . . .
Is there a ghost of an ancestral treaty
For mutual survival?
As you shared,
And share,
This earth's fragile hospitality?

And what explains the sense of some ancient, hidden
    nature
Overlapping somewhere along the line with man's . . .
A nature venerated in antiquity
When this shape-shifting sea-sprite
Was Poseidon's messenger, a Gaian pilot . . .
A demigod.

All much less quirky, less sentimental
When you are inches away
Looking into its lake-like eye.

The dolphin surges up,
Its head above the water,
Then all of its body,
Tail-walking . . .
Walking on the water . . .
Is it in imitation of your dog-paddling stance, as it
    skitters with its tail;
Or mimicking upright mammals
Glimpsed on the distant shoreline, sauntering along the
    strand;
Or starting a new religion; a Delphic Christianity,
With a tossed-off acrobatic miracle,
Levitating half a ton with a flick of a fan . . . ?

It lowers itself slowly into the water,
Like Excalibur.
And then remains level with your body.

It seems to detect that you are flagging;
Shrouds you with one flipper,
Supports you with another;
Keeping you both afloat
With the eddying wake
From its muscular outboard below.

Your heads are together
Your body grasped and scalloped by its smooth, flat
    arms,
In what feels like an embrace.

You hear the appalled voice of a skeptic friend:
"But where do you think it will *lead* . . . ?
What can it *come* to . . . in the *end?*"
And, as in an unrestrained romance, you ignore the
    question,
Refusing to acknowledge the impossibility . . .

Again, as if in response to thought,
The dolphin breaks away,
Its arms spreading apart in an open gesture:
Supplication . . . ? benediction . . . ? a shrug . . . ?
Its palms outwards, then quizzically turned
And dropped to its side.

You know you are reading too much into the gestures,
But you also know that they are not merely mechanical,
Performed for the benefit of some behaviourist's graph
  of trigger-signals and response,
And if you didn't read them,
You would be blinding yourself to the character of a
  creature,
Who was making itself felt in the world
Long before you were thought of.


The dolphin descends,
Swimming around you, mercurially,
And you pursue it again below.
It whirls and coils,
Describing three-dimensional hieroglyphs in its watery
  space,
Then glances across at you.
A pencil-thin stream of bubbles pours from its blowhole
As it speaks.
Again, you are lost for a reply.
Immersed in this its element,
Knowing less than nothing.

Above the entrance
Of the oracle of its namesake, Delphi,
Was written the salutary phrase: *Gnothee seauton,*
Know thyself.
And all you know
Is that its serene assurance
Suggests that it knows exactly how to be a dolphin,
And few humans have the foresight to be human.

You float back up.
It thrusts itself after you, bursting through the surface
And leaping through the air, like a rainbow, above your
    muddled head
As if accounting it
And its billions of bemused neurons
No more significant than a bobbing buoy.

It plummets
Then rises again, circling you on the surface,
Fixing you with a look
That seems calculated to incinerate all further
    resistance.
It sidles down beneath your legs,
Parting them with its bottle-nose,
And slowly rises,
Deftly tuning itself to your centre of gravity.
As you find a handhold on its dorsal fin
Its muscles tense. It bends its backbone
Levering its flukes up and down
And explodes into action,
Sculling and skimming across the water
Rising and falling like a barrage balloon,

Ten, fifteen, twenty knots—
You gasp for breath
As you are scooped in and out of the water
Trying to kneel, slipping,
A rickety human outrigger,
Drawn along in a tornado of foam,
Swept along in a ferment of physicality,
Thunderously thrashing through the waves,
Shouting ecstatic childish smatterings,
Then buried in the water, then surfacing
And gasping and choking again
As the wind knocks the air back down your lungs
And breathing seems as hard
As drinking water from a fire-hydrant.

The dolphin draws to a halt.
You fall forward beside its blowhole,
Inhaling its warm breath, as you come to rest
In a pool below the cliffs of Ballymacadoyle.

The dolphin lets its mount slip from its back
Planting you near the safety of a rock,
You perch there, ecstatic, as the dolphin glides away,
Clinging to what has just occurred
And cautioning yourself that such feelings, clung to,
Swiftly turn to self regard, and vanish, like fairy gold.

You gaze at the dolphin,
Now carelessly fishing in the private crevices
Of the Eask Peninsula;
Slapping its tail down upon the surface
To change some subaquatic status quo.

As you shiver, repeatedly,
At the bite of a southeasterly wind,
And watch it from the safety of dry land,
Now barrelling through a comfortless quilt of spitting
    waves,
Its life suddenly seems gruesomely austere.

And yet
It is lived out in places
Where a luminous beauty is its daily diet.
At every moment it absorbs the fugitive delicacy
Of its liquid underworld;
An aquanaut, sailing through the landscape
Where from hour to hour
It may never see a single irksome thing.

Raw beauty is a daily rule of life,
Rather than an elitist exception
Fussed and tussled over by investors in art
Who crudely see beauty as the hardest currency there
    is—

The lifeless prop of nest-building pride.

And perhaps, when that incessant, enrapturing beauty
Lying just beneath the surface, free of any price-tag,
Perennially suffuses your whole being
As you move through a world without boxes, or walls, or
    doors, or roads,
With no one ever between you and the sky
Leaping through three dimensions towards whatever
    takes your fancy,
You would be different.

And close to,
Drawn into the dolphin's force-field,
Smitten by the shamanistic glimmer
In an eye that distills a lifelong exposure
To another, rarer state of the world,
You too are alchemically touched
And when asked what it was like
Will find yourself saying: "It was beautiful,"
Unselfconscious of the crashing obviousness of the
    word.

The sun begins to set in the Blasket Sound
Silhouetting the two sugar-loaf shapes
Of Inishvickillane and Inishnabró,
Their fissures fading in the dusk.

The dolphin rises slowly,
Its head lying above the water,
And closes one eye,
Resting alternate halves of its brain;
Never wholly sleeping,
Like the Awakened One,
The sobriquet of the sleepless Buddha.

A boat appears.
An emerging blur along the coastline from Dunquin.
The dolphin opens both eyes
Giving the object an evaluating glance
As it clarifies.

The dolphin whistles softly,
Chirrups,
Opens its blowhole,
Then half closes it to emit a taut, brief trumpet
And clicks.
One sound is repeated,
Slowly seeming more recognisable than the rest:
". . . Offfeee . . . Offfeee . . ."
Not unlike "Dolphin . . . dolphin . . . "
The word that you were shouting earlier,
Uneasily.

It swims towards the boat
Reappearing at the stern, inspecting its propeller,
    circumspectly,
Then leaps high out of the water, above the gunnels,
To glimpse those on board.

A story runs that its parents were caught and drowned
    in bottom nets
And it connects the sound of an engine with their death
Allowing no boat to pass without being closely vetted.

The story runs that years ago,
When the two bodies were brought up on deck,
Their skin cut into, griddled by nylon filaments,
Their eyes pecked out by crabs,
A two-foot dolphin followed the trawler into the bay,
And wriggled beside it, haunting it for months.

The boat approaches.
"All right . . . ?"
"All right."
The meagre exchange seems to accentuate the cold.

"You want a spin . . . ? We're going back."
You clamber aboard,
Your shivering body perfidiously grateful for the ride.
The engine grinds back into gear.
As you gaze wistfully at a plume of incandescent vapour
You hear someone on board drily declare below his
    breath:
". . . Another one quare for the fuckin' dolphin."
And you catch a reciprocal nod of assent and an
    indifferent snort
From his companion, out of the corner of your eye.

You are presently asked if you want a blanket,
And regarded like some disaster victim.
No longer competent. Out of it. Looked at as through
    doubleglazing.

"Treacherous tides," someone adds, flatly,
But with enough emphasis to ensure you know you're
    being rescued.
And a look that says he hopes you know enough to buy
    him a drink.

The boat finds its way past the Towérin Bán,
Entering the blind harbour of Daingean Uí Chús.
And its sheltered leaden lagoon.

You stare back at the horizon and the last black fleck
Of that spirit moving upon the face of the waters;
You catch the peripheral comments of the trawlermen.
"He's a big fish altogether."
"There's a museum that would want him surely . . . ."
"He'll be flushed out soon enough when the harbour's
     dredged."
"Yirra Christ, he should be rid of before then,
He does more damage than the fuckin' seals.
You ever seen his teeth, they'd tear your fuckin' tripes
     out.
He takes a ton of fish a day."

The dolphin has moved towards Valencia,
In the direction of the Atlantic;
At the last glimpse,
Still glowing with that selfless zen smile,
Leaving you to a more familiar cold.
But part of you from now on is out there, all at sea.
And you stand later in a rain-squall
On the Kerry quayside
As bereft as a fish discarded from the daily catch
Mouthing on the concrete;
But with something unaccountable added.
To taste.

# Table Of Contents

# Preface

## Why Did We Do It?

We wrote this book because we had to.

We were both at a point in our lives where we were taking stock—reflecting on who we were and why. Looking over all that we had and all we'd achieved, and asking, "Where do we go from here?"

We'd each come to a crossroads in our journey through life and didn't know how to proceed. Or what to proceed with. More and more, we found ourselves wondering what to bring along and what to leave behind, what to acquire and what to give away, what to do and with whom to do it.

Separately, we each knew we needed to bring a new energy into our lives.

Together, we set off on this project to do so.

We both instinctively felt as if we were carrying too much baggage from the past—but neither of us knew how to lighten the load. The same burdens that weighed upon us were the very ones that had sustained us in our lives so far. Our jobs, our homes, our personal relationships all gave our lives a fullness, but at the same time, often seemed like more than we could bear. We constantly wondered if all we had packed into our lives left any room for really living.

It seemed like we were questioning nearly everything that we had worked for since we were young. Supposedly, the best part of life was already over and all we had to show for it was a faded image of ourselves that wasn't even really who we wanted to be. And certainly not for the long road that lay ahead.

When we started working on this book, Dick was 48 and Dave was 35. We effectively bookended the "baby boom" generation in its collective journey through the years. Our concerns reflected what many of our contemporaries are going through, have gone through, and will continue to go through in the future.

At different ages, we were, as the great Swiss psychoanalyst Carl Jung put it, stepping "into the afternoon of life." We were taking this step with the false assumption that the truths and ideas from the morning of life would still serve us as before. But as Jung cautions, "we cannot live the afternoon of life according to the program of life's morning—for what was great in the morning will be little at evening, and what in the morning was true will at evening have become a lie."

Certainly, neither of us was prepared for what we were getting into as we stepped forward—and right into it. Having developed successful programs for our "mornings," we both felt rather lost as we began journeying through our "afternoons."

Without realizing it, we had given in to our culture's worn-out view of adulthood—that the person you are at mid-life is the person you will be for the rest of your life.

But in writing this book together, we realized we were wrong.

At precisely the time we felt our lives weighing us down, we found ourselves taking unexpected trips of growth and aliveness.

We found out, though, that the program for "afternoon" and on into the evening lies within us. To discover this program, we must turn our gaze inward. To know where we are on the trip, where we want to go, and how to get there, we must learn to count on an inner sense of direction.

*We must unpack and repack our bags.*

Unpacking simply means taking a long, hard look at what we're carrying and why. Seeing if our possessions, responsibilities, and relationships are still helping us move forward, or if they're dragging us down.

Repacking, then, is the ongoing activity of reevaluation and reinvention. Rearranging our priorities. Reframing our vision of the good life. And recovering a new sense of being alive.

Once we began to gaze inward, we realized first, that repacking is a critical life skill. It's a process we must go through over and over in order to keep growing and changing, in order to maintain a sense of purpose and direction in our lives, and in order to keep from falling into patterns that not only don't get us where we're going, but which actually hold us back from where we want to be.

And second, we came to understand that the road ahead can indeed be the best part of the journey. It can be a chance to rediscover and reembrace what matters most to us—an opportunity to attain a deeper and more authentic sense of fulfillment than ever before.

Based on seminars and interviews we have conducted, we are convinced that this time, which is often disparaged as "midlife," has every potential to be the best time of our lives—as long as we're willing to engage in repacking.

This book was written as a chronicle of our own repacking. During the two-plus years we worked on it, we think we each became more fully the person we really are. We both developed a new understanding of what we were really looking for in life and how to go about attaining it. We allowed each other and others to see a little more of who we are, and in doing so, became more visible to ourselves, as well.

We offer this chronicle, then, as a guidebook for our peers and fellow travelers.

May it also help you lighten your load for the rest of your life

## Who Needs This Book?

Do any of these statements sound familiar?

- "I've got to get my life under control."
- "I don't know who I want to be for the rest of my life."
- "I'm not fully living my life."

If so, *Repacking Your Bags: Lighten Your Load for the Rest of Your Life* is for you.

It's particularly appropriate if you find yourself at a place in your life where past patterns are weighing you down. If the person you've always been isn't the person you want to be for the rest of your life.

If you feel like you have most everything a person could want, but are still lacking the one thing everyone needs—fulfillment—then you may find what you're looking for in *Repacking*.

This isn't a book for people who believe that lightening their load means they have to sell all their possessions and move to the woods or an ashram in India. It's for people involved in the day-to-day struggle of juggling work, home, and relationship demands in a manner that enables them to make ends meet while burning the candle at both.

Repacking is for businesspeople, professionals, homemakers, students, and retirees—in short, everyone who needs to prepare for and embrace a transition into the next phase of their lives.

If you're one of the 76 million Americans born between the years 1946 and 1964—the so-called Baby Boomers—*Repacking* may have special appeal.

Look around. Most of your contemporaries are no longer

consumed with consumption. Hardly anyone still believes that the "most toys" wins. Accumulation is no longer the name of the game—your friends and colleagues are now asking: "What really matters?" "How much is enough?" and "What is the good life and how can I live it?"

*Repacking Your Bags* offers a new life/work model, a fresh way of thinking about what matters most in your life and how to attain it.

There are hundreds of books out there on job hunting. On résumé writing. On money management. On career planning. The topics are virtually endless, but most share an assumption that life can be compartmentalized. Most put forth the position that people can work on an element of their lives independently of other factors.

*Repacking Your Bags* takes a radically different approach— radical in its simplicity. Instead of breaking things down into parts, the book focuses on reintegration of the whole. It's about putting it all back together. Instead of viewing life as a collection of compartments, it takes a "whole person" approach that takes into account four elements critical to a successfully integrated life—*work, love, place, and purpose.*

*Repacking* starts with an assumption that seems obvious, but which is too often overlooked: everyone has a different definition of "success." Therefore, in order to achieve an authentic experience of our own success, each of us must introspect. *Repacking* offers an approach to do that—an approach that is unique in three ways.

First, by providing a generic formula for the good life into which you can plug your own specifics, *Repacking* enables you to shape your own vision of what the good life means to you, personally.

Second, *Repacking* encourages you to reflect on and commit to your vision of the good life through an emphasis on dialogue— with yourself and others.

Third, *Repacking* uses the metaphor of travel—and baggage—to help remind you that life is a journey and that your experience on the way is inextricably bound up in the baggage—emotional, intellectual, and physical—that you are carrying.

Essentially, it's about choice—fundamental choice—but choice that springs from inner needs and a lifetime perspective.

To put it another way, *Repacking Your Bags* can help you have a mid-life crisis on purpose.

Your life can change radically, without having to change everything in your life. Without having to move to the woods or make a pilgrimage to that ashram in India.

In the course of writing this book, we've both engaged in a good deal of repacking ourselves, so we know that it works. This isn't to say that it's easy—but it is to say that if we can do it, so can you.

The ability to repack our bags and make choices that move us in new, more fulfilling directions is a power that lies within us all. The writing of *Repacking Your Bags* has helped us do that, and we hope that your experience with *Repacking* can do the same for you.

Richard J. Leider
*Minneapolis, Minnesota*

David A. Shapiro
*Seattle, Washington*

*October, 1994*

# The Question That Started It All . . .

*"Life cannot be hurried."*
— MAASAI SAYING

## The Question That Started It All . . .

Dick explains how it all began.

Late one afternoon, on a trek through the highlands along the edge of the Serengeti Plains in East Africa, I experience a breakthrough.

It is a year in which East Africa is suffering one of the worst droughts in history. The vast plains are parched, stripped to dust. River beds run bone dry. Fields of lush grass have been reduced to crabbed patches of stiff straw, and the myriad flowers, normally painted in deep shades of green, blue, and mauve, are bleached of all color. Only the dust devils, whirling high overhead and then touching down on the hard, fractured ground seem to prosper.

In the distance, over the scorched Serengeti, move incredible herds of animals—more than 3 million strong—coming together in search of water and food, tracing the hoof-worn trails that are the highways of their migratory route. They pour steadily across the plains in a broad stream several miles long. It is an extraordinary spectacle, unlike anything else on earth.

The sun is setting, creating water mirages that appear and disappear before our eyes. But the intense heat lingers like a bad dream. It has drained us of all energy. We ride along in our Land Rover, like so many rag dolls strapped in our seats. Small cracks in the vehicle's frame vacuum in clouds of dust that blanket us. The fine silt seeps into our pores until our own bodies feel as dry as the surrounding terrain.

As the leader of this group of twelve mid-life adventurers who have traveled 7000 miles on this "Inventure Expedition" to come face to face with Africa and themselves, I feel especially exhausted. The responsibility of assuring their safety and continued involvement in our process is at times, almost as oppressive as the heat.

We pull into Magaduru, a small Maasai village in the highlands above the Serengeti. We will be camping here for the night before the start of our backpacking trek in the morning.

A tall, lean Maasai man of aristocratic bearing springs upon our vehicles. He plunges the shaft of his spear into the ground and stands in the pose of the heron, balancing on one foot, bracing the other on the inner thigh of the supporting leg. He adjusts the small sword that hangs on his waist, then throws a worn blanket around his body, with a confidence that imparts style and grace to this simple gesture. His dark, penetrating eyes survey us as if scouting the windswept plain that lies behind. No emotion is revealed on his proud, serious face.

Then suddenly, he breaks into a broad smile and greets us in a combination of English and Kiswahili.

"*Jambo*! Welcome to my *boma*!"

He talks rapidly with our guide, David Peterson, fixing

his gaze first on us, then nodding in the direction of his nearby cattle. Loud laughter erupts from the bushes where women and children are hiding.

"What is he saying?" we ask.

David smiles. "He hopes the smell of cattle dung is not too strong for you!"

This breaks the ice. Our laughter fills the air, joining that of our greeter. He introduces himself as Thaddeus Ole Koyie, the village chief. Gripping my hands firmly, he invites our group to be his guests.

In the lively conversation that follows, Koyie, who will be our Maasai guide for the upcoming trek, tells us that he has been educated at missionary school, where he learned to speak English. He does not explain, though, why he has turned his back on "modern" ways. Clearly, he is an influential chief, particularly for a man who is only forty. But there is something more and it implies a powerful sense of place and deep contentment with village life.

The Maasai are intensely communicative in the company of people they know. For reasons of their own, however, they are aloof and suspicious toward strangers. Happily, we don't remain strangers for long.

All of us are quite taken with Koyie. A gregarious and witty man, he has the uncanny ability to move easily between the two worlds of our group and his village, transcending the barriers of language and custom. That night, around the small campfire, when he speaks of the drought, tears glisten in his eyes. Through his passionate eloquence, we come to understand that drought, to the Maasai, is very nearly a death sentence.

Early next morning, as we leave Koyie's *boma* on our trek, I proudly sport a brand-new backpack. It is one of those high-tech ultralight models designed for maximum cargo-carrying efficiency. You know the kind—covered with snaps, clasps, and zippers, full of pockets and pouches, compartments inside compartments, a veritable Velcro heaven—and I have the thing stuffed. I'm a walking advertisement for a Patagonia or L.L. Bean catalogue. But of course, I have to be. As expedition leader, I'm responsible for the entire group. So, in addition to the required group-size first aid kit, I've also been sure to bring along items that will make our trek not just safe, but enjoyable. I'm no Boy Scout, but I certainly subscribe to their motto, "Be prepared." And I have made it a point to be prepared for just about anything.

As we walk along, Koyie keeps glancing at my pack. Time and again, I see him mentally comparing the heavy load I carry with his own, which consists of nothing more than a spear and a stick used for cattle tending. Eventually we get to talking about my backpack, and he expresses his fascination with seeing its contents. Pleased at how impressed he appears to be, I offer to show him my stuff. I look forward to letting him see how carefully I've prepared for our journey and how ready I am for anything.

The opportunity presents itself late that afternoon as we are setting up camp near another *boma*. Proudly, I commence to lay out for him everything in my pack. I unsnap snaps, unzip zippers, and un-Velcro Velcro. From pouches, pockets, and compartments I produce all sorts of strange and wonderful items. Eating utensils, cutting devices, digging tools. Direction finders, star gazers, map readers. Things to write with and on. Various garments in various sizes for various functions. Medical supplies, remedies, and cures. Little bottles inside little bottles inside little bottles. Waterproof bags for everything. Amazing stuff!

At length, I have all the gear spread out. It looks like that photo they always have in the centerfold of the great explorer article that shows everything necessary for a successful trip to the farthest reaches of the planet. Needless to say, I'm pretty satisfied with my collection.

I look over at Koyie to gauge his reaction. He seems amused, but silent. I understand. Surveying the items arrayed about us, I don't know quite what to say, either.

Finally, after several minutes of just gazing at everything, Koyie turns to me and asks very simply, but with great intensity:

*"Does all this make you happy?"*

There was something very powerful about Koyie's question. His words seemed to hit right at the heart of my deepest values. I honestly couldn't answer him that evening, and even weeks afterwards, I couldn't completely say for sure.

In a split second, his question had gotten me to think about all that I was carrying and why—not just on our trek, but through my entire life.

Compelled by a need to explain it to Koyie—and myself—I immediately began going through all that I had, trying to decide if it *did* make me happy. He and I sat around the fire and talked long into the night. As he listened to me, I listened also, for I found that I was clarifying the core values of my life.

In response to the question, I began to realize the truth. Some of the things did make me happy, but many of them didn't—at least not in any way that made sense to be dragging them along. So as I repacked, I set those things aside, and eventually, gave them to the local villages. I went on the rest of the trek without them. I'm not sure that I'll never want or need them again, but I certainly didn't suffer for not having them at the time.

My load was much lighter after I'd reexamined my needs. And on the rest of the trip, I was quite a bit happier for having repacked my bags.

As a result of this experience, I began to assemble my thoughts and feelings about how to *lighten my load*. The insight I've gained has contributed to and been informed by my work as a life and career planning counselor. In discussions with clients, colleagues, and family members, I've developed a new understanding of how important it is to periodically *unpack* and *repack* our bags at various points in our lives.

As my co-author, David, and I have worked with these thoughts, we've made a number of discoveries that are at the core of this book:

- We've discovered that many people are laboring through their lives, weighed down by attachments that no longer serve them. Patterns of behavior that have helped them get where they are, aren't helping them get where they want to be. As a result, many people feel desperate. They are grieving over the loss of a life—their own. In order to overcome this despair—which we all feel at certain points in our lives—we must confront it, and quite literally, laugh in its face. This is what we look at in *Section I: Does All This Make You Happy?*

- We've discovered that it is possible to simplify one's life without sacrificing the conveniences and comforts we've come to expect. We can *give up* without *giving in*. By having less *in* our lives, we can get more *out of* life. To get to this place, we have to figure out what really matters. We have to examine what's in our bags and decide for ourselves if it's really what we want—and ought—to be carrying. This is the focus of *Section II: Unpacking Your Bags.*

- We've developed a new appreciation for what the "good life" entails and how important it is that, in creating a vision of the good life for ourselves, we take into account four critical factors: *work, love, place,* and *purpose.* The first three of these are considered in *Section III: Work Bags; Section IV: Relationship Bags;* and *Section V: Finding Your Place.* Purpose is woven in throughout the book.

- We've learned that what we carry "in our bags" defines

how we spend our time. And how we spend our time determines how we live and who we are. Sadly, many of us are laboring in ways that are unrelated to the things we really want to do with our lives. It is entirely possible, though, to redesign our lives—to repack our bags—in order to have, do, and be the person we've always wanted to be. We deal with this issue, and offer suggestions for how to do it in *Section VI: Repacking Your Bags*.

- We've found that happiness has more to do with experiencing than with having. Having is great, but it's not *it*. For most of us, what we're really looking for is a feeling —a feeling of *aliveness*. This is what *Section VII: The Freedom of the Road* is all about.

Over the past few years, Dick's relationship with Koyie has grown—and the learning has continued. The countless conversations they've had sitting around late night fires and trekking across wind-swept plains have given us great insight into ourselves and our culture. Koyie gently reminds us that the freedom to choose is not something we *have* and therefore can lose, but something we *are*. It is of our deepest essence, just waiting to be called upon.

At every moment, in every situation, we are free to choose a simpler expression of our being. We always have the potential to unpack, lighten our loads, and repack.

For many of us it takes a crisis, mid-life or other, to get us even thinking about what we're carrying. And then, unfortunately, we tend to make decisions from within the crisis. Instead of pausing to reconsider, in a purposeful manner, what we've brought along and why, we're apt to cast everything off and just run. Instead of making rational decisions that prepare us for what's ahead, we tend to come from a position of panic or fear— and the choices we make reflect that.

We can use a process for repacking our bags to stimulate thought on this issue outside of a crisis. We can reflect on our lives in a manner that helps us sort out what's really important—what makes us happy—from what's just weighing us down. We can then map out a new road ahead, one that will get us where we really want to go, with the things we really want to bring along the way.

And that, in a nutshell—or should we say backpack—is what this book is all about.

The process is not something that we experience once and are done with. It's an experience, like Koyie's question, that stays with you, that stimulates thinking and inspires ongoing reflection. We hope you'll find it useful and meaningful no matter where you currently are in life.

There are many ways to engage the process, and you'll discover your own as you proceed. But perhaps the best way to get going is to begin with the question that started it all:

*"Does all this make you happy?"*

# Does
# All This
# Make You
# Happy?

# CHAPTER 1

# Refinding Your Smile

*"Pack up your troubles in your old kit-bag*
*And smile, smile, smile."*
— GEORGE ASAF, 1915

## It's 9:00 A.M. Do You Know Where Your Smile Is?

In the movie *City Slickers*, Billy Crystal plays Mitch Robbins, a disillusioned radio advertising salesperson who takes a much-needed vacation at a Western dude ranch with a couple of long-time friends. At the beginning of the film, he considers whether he really wants to go—what with all the daily trials and tribulations of his life, he thinks the trip will be more trouble than it's worth. His wife disagrees, explaining why she thinks it's so necessary that he get away.

"You need to go find your smile," she tells him. She insists that rediscovering his sense of humor matters more than anything else he's doing at the time.

She's right. And over the course of the film, Mitch learns this too. He comes to understand the value of laughter and what a difference it makes to have a smile in one's heart. At the end of the movie, nothing in his life has changed, but everything has. He still has the same job, the same family, the same problems, but having refound his smile, is able to embrace them with a renewed sense of joy.

Many people today are in the same place Mitch was at the start of the film. They've lost their smiles. There's little or no joy in their hearts. The days ahead look flat and repetitive, as boring and monotonous as high school math class. Faced with this prospect of endless replication, people "lose their edge." They feel dull—and dulled. They feel trapped, insulated. They "go through the motions," of living, but there's no life in their lives.

More and more, we hear friends and associates say, "I'm so overwhelmed these days. I just don't know how to have fun anymore."

That's not quite true. For many people, "fun" has become an addiction. But as with most addictive substances, people build up a tolerance to it. So despite all the "fun" things people do, they're still not having fun.

What's really missing is a sense of joy. People find that they no longer feel an authentic joyfulness in living, despite all the fun stuff they have or do. And this is the case whether they're male or female, young or old, rich or poor, no matter what stage of life they are in.

What's happened to people is that they've lost a delicate, but critical component of aliveness and well being—they've lost their *eccentricities*. It happens to many of us in early adulthood. We fit in. We see how other people survive and we copy their style — same as everyone else. Swept along by the myriad demands of day-to-day living, we stop making choices of our own. Or even realizing that we have choices to make.

We lose the wonderful weird edges that define us. We cover up the eccentricities that make us unique. Alfred Adler, the great 20th century psychologist and educator, considered these eccentricities a vital part of a happy and fulfilling lifestyle. Ironically, the very term he coined—lifestyle—has come to imply something almost entirely opposed to eccentricity. It's turned out to mean a preconfigured package, formatted for easy consumption. Lifestyle now relates to things that we buy—someone else's idea of what we need to be happy. But is anyone really satisfied with these mass-marketed ideas of happiness? Is anyone really nourished by a McLifestyle?

It's no wonder so many people feel they've lost their smiles. But more poignantly, how many would even notice if they found them?

## Why Do We Feel So Bad?

*Forbes* magazine—"the capitalist's tool," no less—devoted its entire 75th anniversary issue to the question, "Why do we feel so bad . . . when we have it so good?" Some of the country's finest writers offered opinions on why so many of us feel so depressed despite having opportunities that our ancestors could only dream about. Their writings echoed a common theme: We're unhappy because something is missing in our lives, something that all the fancy gadgets and fun toys in the world can't replace.

Lifestyle choices surround us, beckoning from glossy magazines and flashy commercials. Despite all these choices, few of us really feel much freedom to choose. There's little sense of creative expression. We're always *going somewhere,* never *being anywhere.* As soon as we do opt for something, it begins to chafe . . . because it never really fit us in the first place. We get trapped into thinking we'll be happy if we behave a certain way, live a certain lifestyle, and purchase all the products that go along with it.

Everywhere you look, you see people pursuing happiness as if it were something they could capture and cage. But pinning happiness down only destroys it. It's too wild for that—it needs room to roam. You have to give it time, let it wander, surprise you.

Dave tells a story about how he learned this the hard—but funny—way:

> It's not just glossy lifestyles people grab for. Instead, some of us try to copy slightly more tarnished images—but with just as predictable results.

The lifestyle I lusted after was the Henry Miller meets Jim Morrison expatriate poet/writer, eking out a living on the fringes of society. I wanted an alternative lifestyle, but I didn't want to have to invent my own alternatives.

So a few years ago, I moved to Paris and bought into the whole tortured artist scene. I dressed only in black and even took up smoking cigarettes to complete the picture. It was all very serious—and when I look back at it now, all very pretentious and boring. There was one moment, though, when my dark veneer of self importance sustained a major—and truly enlightening—crack.

I was sitting in a cafe, nursing a glass of Bordeaux, affecting a pose of resigned world weariness. I observed the passersby outside on the street going through the pointless motions of human life, and my heart was filled with deep existential despair. A small dog appeared, and while I watched, deposited a large turd on the sidewalk just in front of the cafe entrance. It seemed to me to be the perfect metaphor for the filth and degradation of everyday existence.

I ordered another glass of wine and resolved to sit and watch until someone stepped into the mess, feeling that this would sum up perfectly how we move through our days—blithely wandering along until, all of a sudden, and for no reason at all, we are soiled with foul and noxious excrement.

The show turned out to be quite amusing—and exciting as hell. Person after person would almost step into it, but at the last second, either notice and move aside, or just miss it. It was like watching a daredevil high-wire act at the circus. I started to have a great time. I was smiling, laughing out loud. I even stopped smoking.

The owner of the cafe, who had always seemed to me to be this forbidding character, came over to me, lured by my good humor. We got into a great conversation about philosophy and American baseball. He introduced me to his wife, who, after remarking that I was too thin, went away and returned with a bowl of the most delicious potato stew I had ever tasted. The owner broke out a special bottle of wine that we shared with great conviviality. I talked to more people that evening than I had in five months. And somewhere along the line, forgot all about my artistic angst.

I ended up closing down the cafe, and after bidding a fond adieu to my new friends, stepped merrily out the door . . . and right into the pile of dog-do. The joke was on me—literally.

That was the loudest I laughed all night. I had refound my smile, and it stayed with me the rest of my trip.

## Pre-Packaged Lifestyles

Like Dave with his ready-to-wear *angst* and off-the-shelf torment, most of us try, at one point or another, to buy into a prepackaged lifestyle we think will make us happy. Just look at the catalogues we get in the mail. You've got your choice of *J. Crew's* sensitive urban professional. Or *L.L. Bean's* semi-reconstructed rural pioneer. *The Sharper Image's* early-adopting techno-whiz with plenty of disposable income. Automobiles, theoretically, provide the same easy answers. There's a certain kind of person who drives a Volvo. He or she wouldn't be caught dead behind the wheel of a Toyota. Nor would that person ever consent to drive their father's Oldsmobile.

Prepackaged lifestyles let someone else—usually someone fictional—do our living for us. The promise, which is also the curse, is that we can slip on a new lifestyle, including the emotions that go along with it, as easily as slipping on a new item of clothing.

The images that go along with prepackaged lifestyles are

always successful ones. Models in the catalogues are always smiling and laughing. They're trim and fit. Characters on our television shows are—if not always glamorous—at least funny, and sure of themselves. The message is that their prepackaged lifestyles *work*. So when it doesn't work for us, we don't question the lifestyle, we question ourselves.

We think, "Oh, I just need something else, one more thing and *then* I'll be happy." It's the catalogue-shopping approach to the good life. The problem is that every few weeks (or around the holidays, every other day), there's a fresh crop of new catalogues. So we're kept in a constant state of unfulfilled desire. The things we buy don't satisfy us, but we keep grabbing for more. We're addicted to accumulation, but our tolerance level is so high that enough is never enough.

No wonder so many people see their own lives described in *The Overworked American*, the best-seller by Harvard University economist Juliet Schor. As she points out, since mid-century, when given the choice, Americans have consistently opted for higher salaries and more money over more time for leisure and family. Yet has this made us any happier? Polls indicate the answer is no. Thus, she notes, we are trapped on a treadmill of more work, more consumer goods, and more destruction of the earth.

And on that treadmill, what happens to one's smile? Well, look around. See the expression so many people wear: half grimace, half fear. Lots of us look like we just ate a bad burrito—with great determination. We're not sure what's going to happen, but we're damn sure not going to let it affect us.

Many of us who have worked hard our entire careers reach a point, usually about middle age, when we examine our lives and say, "Hey! Is this all there is? When does the fun start?" The problem for many people today is that they've never really developed their own vision of success. They've assumed that if they just bought into someone else's image of what it means to be happy, they'd be happy, too. It's as if they think they can find their smiles by buying a clown mask. But that doesn't change anything. And like the old song says, it doesn't hide the tears when no one's around.

## Refinding Your Smile

In the 18th century, Sebastian Chamfort wrote, "The most wasted day is one in which we have not laughed." How many days have you wasted recently? When was the last time you had a real good belly laugh?

Editor and writer Norman Cousins, explained in his best-seller, *Anatomy of an Illness*, how laughter helped him overcome the pain of his severely debilitating disease of the endocrine system. "I made the joyous discovery that ten minutes of genuine belly laughter had an anesthetic effect and would give me at least two hours of pain-free sleep." Part of the therapy he designed for himself included watching Marx Brothers' movies and reading humor books.

Cousins noted only one negative side effect of his laughter when he was in the hospital—it disturbed the other patients. No doubt because they weren't laughing themselves. It's too bad he didn't have a big-screen TV, because sharing laughter is even better than laughing alone. Two smiles—like two heads—are better than one.

Humor is a gift to both receiver *and* giver. Stand-up comics talk about getting addicted to the rush that comes from performing. "Making a whole room of people laugh is better than sex," says comic Ralf Leland. "But then again, I've never had sex with a whole room."

Laughter made Norman Cousins feel better physically, but there's another sense of feeling better, too. Regular doses of laughter also make you *better at feeling*. A good belly laugh loosens you up. It brings all your emotions closer to the surface.

People who are quick to laugh strike us as lively and warm-hearted. Thomas Carlyle, the 19th century English philosopher, said that no one "who has laughed heartily and wholly can be altogether irreclaimably bad." On the other hand, humorless people usually seem severe and uptight. It's hard for us to imagine a group of stiff-collared Pilgrims slapping their knees and yukking it up. We tend to envision their lives as emotionally limited—not too hot, not too cold. Under control. Laughter has a way of breaking down that control. It's subversive. Nothing like a pie in the face to bring a big-shot back down to size.

We all can use a little subversion in our own lives. We can all stand to have a little air let out of our inflated egos. In Shakespeare's Midsummer Night's Dream, the wood-nymph Puck, that "merry wanderer of the night," delights in poking fun at old gossips, and wise aunts, and other pompous self-important types. He tells how his antics make whole crowds of people "hold their hips and laugh and waxen in their mirth, and neeze and swear. A merrier hour was never wasted there."

How many merry hours have you wasted lately?

If you can laugh at yourself, it changes your whole mood. Think of that the next time you're rushing madly around in the morning, desperate to get to work. Step back and try to see the humor in the situation. Imagine yourself in one of those old time silent comedies. What would the Keystone Kops have to say about your character?

## Tips for Refinding Your Smile

You know the feeling you get when you look over your old high school yearbook? It's an odd mixture of relief and regret coupled with a certain disbelief that you ever could have been there or done that. As you repack your bags you'll probably have similar feelings. What will sustain you though, and make it an enjoyable as well as rewarding experience, will be your ability to see the lighter side of the choices you made. If you can hang on to your smile, you'll do a better job of repacking and just as importantly, have more fun while doing so.

As a wrap-up to this part of the process and warm-up for what comes next, here are a few additional tips and suggestions for refinding your smile. As you move on through this book and afterwards, we encourage you to revisit them whenever you need a lift.

- *Prime your smile.*

  It's easier to keep laughing than to start. So treat yourself to things you find funny as a means to get your laughter engine going. Rent some Marx Brothers or Three Stooges movies, or listen to a few tapes by George Carlin, Lily Tomlin, or Robin Williams.

- *Laugh, and the whole world laughs with you.*

  Laughter has its roots in shared experience. So schedule a dinner party or a picnic to be with people who make you laugh and, more importantly, who find your jokes funny.

- *Play with kids.*

  Kids are funny, and they know it. If you spend some time with them—playing, as opposed to trying to make them clean their rooms or whatever—you're certain to find a laugh or three.

- *Wear an odd article of clothing.*

  Put on a loud tie, a silly hat, a patterned shirt that amuses you. It may not seem like much, but it's pretty hard to stay morose, when you look at yourself in the mirror and see Mickey Mouse staring back from between your lapels.

- *Rekindle a romance.* (Preferably your own.)

  The world tends to look a little brighter when you're in love. It's easier to laugh off a traffic jam or missed connecting flight when you're sitting next to someone you really care about. So take the opportunity to rediscover your core connection to the person or people to whom you're most attached. Spend some time alone and recall some of the best laughs you've had together—literally. Act them out. Retell the old jokes. Share the wonderful absurdity of caring deeply for one another. If you can find the humor in your closest personal relationships, you can find the humor in anything.

- *Take something incredibly seriously.*
  The hardest you ever laugh is when you're not supposed to—like during a slumber party after Dad comes in and tells you all to be quiet or else. Use this same strategy on something in your life today, preferably something that's pretty absurd to begin with. Professional wrestling would be perfect. If you can see the seriousness of something silly, it can help you turn things around and see the lighter side of something really serious, too.

- *Enroll in a stand-up comedy or theater improvisation or storytelling class.*
  Check out your local comedy clubs or community theaters. Most probably offer some kind of introductory comedy class. Enrolling doesn't guarantee you'll become the next Lily Tomlin, but it is a safe bet you'll get a lot of laughs out of the experience.

- *Learn to tell at least one joke.*
  Lots of people claim they can't tell jokes—all that means is they *don't*. But it doesn't take any special talent to be funny. It just takes practice. So, check some joke books out of the library and inflict them on your friends. Sure, they'll groan when you treat them to a clunker, but you know they'll be telling the same joke to their friends first chance they get.

- *Call in well.*
  There's nothing quite so delicious as playing hooky. So "call in well" to work one day and just take it easy. Go

see a comedy matinee at your local movie theater. Sit in a restaurant at lunch time and revel in the joy of being "bad" for a day.

- *Do one "deviant" thing a day for the next ten days.* Why be normal? Dare to be different. Way different. Resolve to do one out-of-the-ordinary thing every day for the next ten days. It can be as mundane as taking a different route to work. Or as wild as dressing in a gorilla suit and terrorizing your office. The point is to shake things up. Deviate from your norm. Get out of the routine. See how it feels to do things in a new and different way.

# Funny Postcards

Mitch Robbins refound his smile, and you can too. Here is a short "Postcard" exercise to get you thinking about ways to do so.

### A Note on Postcards and Dialogue

This, and the other postcard exercises in the book, are designed to remind you that life is a journey, and that it's important to include others in it. To let them know where you are. And how things are going on the way.

Postcards are an especially quick and easy way to correspond with friends, family, and colleagues. It's a lot less intimidating to write a postcard than to sit down and craft a handwritten letter. And often, it's just as effective. Usually, reaching out to make contact is what matters. It's not necessarily *what* you say, but simply that you *say* it. It's about getting the dialogue going.

Dialogue lies at the very foundation of all Western culture. Our religious and philosophical beliefs are rooted in dialogue. Ironically, though, one of the most common complaints we hear about contemporary society is that *no one talks anymore.*

Friends, clients, business associates all echo the same refrain. No one has time for real heart-to-heart talk. And when we do get together to talk, it's about *things*—work, sports, fashion, TV. Anything to keep the conversation light and lively and away from what's really going on. Meanwhile, what we really want to talk about is life—our lives—in depth.

Nietzsche wrote about "marriage as a long conversation." Many marriages quickly descend into short-tempered comments, or just as often, total silence.

The same goes for many work relationships. The two most meaningful dialogues most people have with anyone at their work are their initial interview and their exit interview. In between, they're too busy hurrying through each day.

Meanwhile, people *really* want to talk. They need to. It's a human instinct as powerful as hunger or thirst. We all need to tell our story and have it be heard.

That's why this book puts such an emphasis on dialogue. The exercises and activities around unpacking and repacking are intended to be done with a partner, or partners, and to stimulate discussion about the issues in question. Consider them a map for your conversations, but don't hesitate to stray off the beaten path if that's where they take you. This isn't to say that you can't do the exercises on your own. Going through the process of completing them will definitely make a difference. But if you can get a dialogue going with someone else, someone who can reflect back to you what you've expressed, you'll learn more about yourself than you would otherwise. And probably have more fun doing so, too.

So we really encourage you to *send* the postcards you write. Use them to get a dialogue going with your postcard penpal.

Choose your postcard penpal—what we call your Dialogue Partner—based on the subject of the postcard you're sending. This means you might have a number of different Dialogue Partners. That's okay. But it's also okay if you only have one or two.

To create your postcards, you can photocopy the postcard

form we've included, and then, after filling it out, fold the two halves over to make a single card for sending. If you prefer (or if you're shy about your mail carrier reading your postcard), drop your postcard in an envelope before sending. If you don't feel like photocopying the form, use an index card or any small piece of paper to write a short message. The key word is "short." Each postcard is meant to be a quick note, a "snapshot" of where you are. Don't agonize over a long involved letter that you'll never get around to finishing. Focus instead on a simple, straightforward message that opens the door to further dialogue.

The postcards can be a catalyst for conversation—like when you send a postcard to someone and then visit them after your trip and see the postcard on their refrigerator. It reminds you of the experience, and gives you a chance to fill in the details. A chance to get a real dialogue going about what happened and how you felt about it. Dialogue that sure beats the standard "Weather's fine. Wish you were here" type of conversations we usually have.

# Postcard Exercise

## Where's Your Smile?

First, think about the following:

1. Are you living your own vision of the good life, or somebody else's?

☐ my own ☐ someone else's ☐ a combination

2. Have you lost or found your smile?

☐ lost ☐ found ☐ neither

3. Are you having more or less fun than you did five years ago?

☐ more ☐ less ☐ about the same

Now, create the Postcard.

4. Pick a person in your life who puts a smile on your face, someone you think would get a kick out of knowing they put a smile on your face. On the front of the card, create an image of how they make you smile. Do a collage, make a sketch, spill coffee, whatever. On the back of the card, write a message to that person. Tell them about the characteristics you've illustrated on the front of the card.

5. Send the card to this Dialogue Partner. Wait for them to respond, or if you don't hear from them in about a week or so, call up and see what they think.

# CHAPTER 2

# What Is the Good Life?

*"The good life is a process, not a state of being.*
*It is a direction, not a destination."*
— CARL ROGERS

## Redefining The Good Life

How do you define the good life?

In his comprehensive work, *The Psychology of Happiness*, Oxford University psychologist Michael Argyle concludes, "The conditions of life which really make a difference to happiness are those covered by three sources—social relations, work, and leisure. And the establishment of a satisfying state of affairs in these spheres does not depend much on wealth, either absolute or relative."

In *The Power of Myth*, Joseph Campbell wrote, "You may have a success in life, but then just think of it—what kind of life was it? What good was it—you've never done the thing you wanted to do in all your life . . . go where your body and soul want to go. When you have the feeling, then stay with it, and don't let anyone throw you off."

For most people, the core of the good life is gaining more control over their time, without letting anyone throw them off. They want time to feed their souls.

A banker and former rock promoter quits his career to start a log building business.

A human performance consultant moves his business and a dozen colleagues to a small town in the mountains to create an intentional community.

A creative director at a successful marketing communications firm, fed up with the inter-office politics at her job, leaves to start her own agency, and within several months, is already competing successfully against her old employers for lucrative contracts.

A middle-aged, middle-manager in an international chemical products company takes part in a two-week outdoor experience trek. He comes back to his job revitalized and excited about simplifying his life and retiring early and starting up a second career.

Mitch Robbins returns from his trail ride carrying a calf. He's heading back to his same old job, same old home, same old life. Nothing has changed, but everything has.

These career and lifestyle choices are triggered by changes in the perception of what it means to live the good life.

Often, the search for the good life is depicted as a fleeing the rat race back-to-the-land scenario, or as spurred by a crisis psychology, neither of which suits our purpose here. For us, the solution is not to be found by running from the rat race or from ourselves, but rather, in unpacking, repacking, and lightening our day-to-day loads.

Helen and Scott Nearing called it an "affirmation." They saw the good life as a way of conducting themselves, of looking at the world and taking part in its activities so as to provide for the values they considered essential to the good life. For them, these values included simplicity, freedom from anxiety or tension, an opportunity to be useful and to live harmoniously.

When we ask people to envision their ideal futures, they almost always see images of nature. More than 90% respond that they see a greater degree of daily contact with the outdoors— parks, oceans, mountains, forests, gardens, sunshine.

As we travel the country today listening to people talk about their vision of the good life, we are amazed at the number of people who are curious about how to simplify their lives. They feel out of control. They find themselves driven by a deep urge to find more time for the important things in their lives. Many, however, don't know where to begin.

The good life means walking the path of integrity. Integrity is derived from the Latin word *integer,* meaning "whole." What is missing from many people's lives is wholeness. The quest for the good life is a quest for wholeness.

We define integrity as "keeping the small promises you make to yourself." There are many paths that lead us toward keeping the small promises and wholeness. But the real good life requires that we understand an even deeper meaning of these words.

In Erik Erikson's view of the stages of the life cycle, the later period of our lives tends to be a time of great inner tension between hope and despair. Erikson observes that eventually, we will look back on what we have done and how we have lived. How we have demonstrated "integrity" in our lives will determine what we will feel—hope or despair.

John Gardner, in *The Recovery of Confidence,* puts it another way: "The cure for boredom is not diversion, it is to find some work to do, something to care about." Because how we live the next phase of our lives is not just a question of personal lifestyle but of what we care about, we define the good life as an integration of *place, love, work,* and *purpose.*

## A Simple Formula for What's Not So Simple

To put it simply, the formula for the good life is:

*Living in the Place you belong, with the People you Love, doing the Right Work, on Purpose.*

What does this mean? Above all, it means an *integration.* A sense of harmony among the various components in one's life. It means, for example, that the place you live provides adequate opportunities for you to do the kind of work you need to do. That your work gives you time to be with the people you really love. And that your deepest friendships contribute to the sense of community you feel in the place you live and work.

The glue that holds the good life together is purpose. Defining your sense of purpose—the reason you get up in the morning—enables you to continually travel in the direction of your vision of the good life. It helps you keep focusing on where you want to go and discovering new roads to get there.

We understand the good life, therefore, as a journey. It's not something we achieve once and hold onto forever. It keeps changing throughout our lives. The balance among place, love, and work is always shifting. At some stages, we'll be especially focused on work issues. At others, we'll be more concerned with developing a sense of place, putting down roots, building a home for ourselves. And all of us know what it's like to have love as our number one concern—maybe all too well.

When we're clear about our purpose, though, it's easier to establish and maintain the necessary sense of balance. Purpose is what keeps us from getting too far sidetracked by issues related to place, love, or work. It provides perspective and a beacon to keep us on the path we've chosen for ourselves. And a way to find ourselves if we start getting too lost.

Mary Anne Wilder, a successful medical products salesperson, sees her purpose as her guiding light. "I've always thought that my real purpose in life is to be a teacher. To help others understand things that I understand already—things that can help them. That's always seemed to me pretty much the reason I'm here. I originally went into sales because I believed I could introduce my customers to solutions they didn't know about beforehand—solutions to make them more effective, to make their lives easier.

"In my career, which is a little over a decade now, I've moved all around the world, have had a number of different relationships—some good, some bad, some neither—and have often almost entirely lost myself in my work. But what's kept me sane is that I know why I'm doing this. I'm still trying to help people learn. And believe it or not, sometimes succeeding.

"I think if I lost that sense—the sense that I am on purpose—I'd have to find something else to do. Or else be a ski-bum for the rest of the my life."

## Defining the Good Life

*Living in the Place you belong,*
*with the People you Love,*
*doing the Right Work,*
*on Purpose.*

Oddly enough, we find that people who have achieved a harmonious relationship among the three areas of work, love, and place become increasingly less anxious about each of them individually. Their concerns about status usually diminish. Their self-confidence and faith in themselves seems to grow. They tend to see the universe as a more benevolent place, and one in which they can exercise a satisfying degree of autonomy.

John Cowan, author, consultant, and Episcopal priest, describes the good life as "moving from anxiety to faith to release." He sees himself as shifting from constant worry about his job, his romantic life, and home to finally, a point where he can let go of his anxieties and frustrations, confident that what he is doing, where he is doing it, and who he is doing it for are all in accord.

If this sounds a little bit on the spiritual side, that's because it is. As we mature, our underlying spiritual concerns cannot help but begin coming to the fore. As Jung put it, "Among all my patients in the second half of life—that is to say over 35—there has not been one whose problem in the last resort was not that of finding a religious outlook on life. It is safe to say that every one of them fell ill because he had lost that which the living religions of every age have given to their followers, and none of them has been really healed who did not regain his religious outlook."

Thus, scores of mid-lifers are choosing to trade some of the current externally-focused definitions of the good life for something that comes more from the inside. They are giving up gadgets and baubles in exchange for integrity and wholeness in their lives. They are pursuing a "right livelihood" that enables them not just to make a living, but to create meaningful, sustainable lives. Most are investigating, in one way or another, one or more of the good life components—*place, love, work, and purpose*—as a means of doing this.

We know lots of people—baby-boomers, generally—who have recently committed or made a renewed commitment to a particular place. They've bought land in a part of the country that has always meant a lot to them, and are making a go at living there despite complications like distance from work or lack of familiar services. Or else they've decided not to move from their current home even though peers and contemporaries are leaving in droves. For these people, and others like them, the internal sense of place is too important a part of what the good life means to ignore.

Similarly, many people we know are making work choices that may not be so great for their careers, but which are exactly what they need to do for themselves. A case in point is our friend, Tom Halloran, an attorney in New Mexico, who has repeatedly turned down high-paying offers from major law firms in order to continue doing what for him is the "right work"—being an advocate for Native Americans in the tribal courts of the Southwest.

> I definitely could make a lot more money doing contract law in Albuquerque. But I don't think there's anything they could pay me that would be worth the satisfaction I get already. And besides, what am I going to do with a Mercedes on the roads out here, anyway?

And it's a truism, but it's certainly true—these days, people generally aren't looking for more relationships, they're looking for more out of the relationships they already have. Love is a remarkably delicate commodity, one which seems more precious than ever before. We see a renewed interest on the part of partners and friends we know in making things work—an increased appreciation for the value of the connection, and more willingness to do whatever it takes to grow together rather than grow apart. One of the most touching social events we recently attended was the remarriage of two dear friends, Steve and Linda Cohen. They had gotten divorced about five years earlier, but in the interim, had discovered that they really did love each other after all. Each had undergone serious self-examination and learned that the person they thought they were looking for was right next to them all along. Although they'd been living together for a couple years, they decided they really wanted to celebrate and honor their renewed feelings for each other and so they remarried. And indeed, it really was a celebration, a true lovefest.

All of these are examples of how people are turning inward to develop a new understanding of and appreciation for a vision of the good life that takes into account place, work, and/or love. In developing this vision, they are quite naturally unpacking and repacking each of these bags. And in doing so, they are also quite naturally overcoming the fears that hold so many others back from their own vision of the good life.

## The 4 Deadly Fears

Nowadays, what most people feel when they don't feel anything in particular is fear.

It's easy to see why. The world is a frightening place. Certainly, the popular media do nothing to disabuse us of the notion. Television, movies, and radio talk shows all remind us to be scared. Very scared. It's as if we're being told that the one natural emotion to feel is a sort of vast, overriding, and amorphous sense of fear.

Our investigations have revealed that though people are indeed fearful, their fear isn't really that vague. In fact, it can be broken down into four main fears, which we call the 4 Deadly Fears because they sap so much life out of us.

The 4 Deadly Fears are:

1. Fear of Having Lived a Meaningless Life

2. Fear of Being Alone

3. Fear of Being Lost

4. Fear of Death

You may be surprised that fear of death isn't at the top of the list. But it turns out that people aren't as afraid of death as you might expect. In fact, it's said that most people are more afraid of speaking in public than they are of dying! Certainly, the first three Deadly Fears we've identified seem to generate more chills than the mere prospect of death.

Note that each of the fears corresponds to one of the four components of the good life in the following way:

| Fear | Good Life Component |
|------|---------------------|
| Fear of Having Lived a Meaningless Life | Work |
| Fear of Being Alone | Love |
| Fear of Being Lost | Place |
| Fear of Death | Purpose |

It's the fear that we'll go to our grave having never made our mark, having never "sung our song," that keeps many of us hard at work. And yet, ironically, it's often the very work that we do, and the responsibilities associated with it, that keep us from ever allowing ourselves to really live.

The fear of being alone drives many of us into a lifelong search for love. But unless we're willing, at some time, to be alone and discover our own individual self, true love with another usually remains forever just out of reach.

Our innate fear of being lost ties many of us to a place, in both literal and figurative terms. And yet who ever really knows where they belong until they've experienced being away from it? How can we ever find ourselves unless we've been lost?

Finally, it's our fear of death that tends to underlie our attempts to infuse our lives with purpose. If we can devote ourselves to a cause or belief larger than ourselves, we can—in some small way—achieve a slice of immortality. But again, as long as we keep seeing purpose as something "out there," instead of something generated from within, we never really achieve an authentic experience of the life that we have. Thus, "achieving" the good life is, in a very real way, a matter of reconciling ourselves to and eventually, overcoming these 4 Deadly Fears.

Establishing and maintaining long-term loving relationships keeps us from feeling alone. As Goethe says, "A life without love, without the presence of the beloved, is nothing but a mere magic-lantern show. We draw out each slide after slide, swiftly tiring of each, and pushing it back to make haste for the next."

Finding our home, creating a sense of place, enables us to stop feeling lost. In the words of Thoreau, "Why has man rooted himself thus firmly in the earth, but that he may rise in the same proportion into the heavens above?"

Doing work we care about in support of something we believe in saves us from feeling that we're wasting our lives. Or, as Bertrand Russell put it, "If you look about you at the men and women whom you can call happy, you will see that they all have certain things in common. The most important of these things is an activity which at most times is enjoyable on its own account, and which, in addition, gradually builds up into something that you are glad to see coming into existence."

Designing the good life becomes, then, "a simple matter" of finding and keeping adequate space for love, place, and work in your life. In other words, reaching for and holding on to what really matters in your life and letting go of the responsibilities and commitments that do not.

# Letting Go

For the past couple decades, Dick has regularly led groups of trekkers on adventure travels to Tanzania, East Africa. Backpacking and sitting around campfires, they talk candidly about their fears, hopes, relationships, work, and futures. The purpose of these trips? To rekindle the fire inside. To unpack. To repack. To rediscover the good life.

Often, after a trip, he will receive letters from fellow trekkers in which the correspondents ask Dick what they should do now that they're back in the "real world." They ask for his advice about packing and repacking. They ask him to tell them what would constitute the good life for them.

Dick's response is to encourage them to listen—not so much to what he has to say—but to themselves. Discovering the good life requires a deeper listening to oneself. A more raw, open and visible relationship to self. Getting there requires continual vulnerability and stepping out from behind the various masks we wear not only in public, but in private, too.

It's a difficult truth—the good life requires personal accountability. No one else can define it for you. The blessing of this is that there's never anyone stopping you from making the effort. The curse is that there's no one stopping you but yourself.

It takes some serious unpacking—letting go—to move forward on the trip. To unpack is to awaken, to see something different, to ask new questions. It is an expression of an urge to create, to live whole.

Time and time again, the world's greatest artists, musicians, sculptors, inventors, scientists, explorers, writers and so forth have testified to the "unpacking" dimension of this creative process. "Regular folks" have too.

Linda Jadwin, a corporate executive with a major technology firm in the Midwest, says: "When I was a young girl, I learned how to swim in a swamp. I was drawn to the mysterious odors and strange textures of its murky depths. I can still remember how it felt to paddle through the cool water while slippery, slimy fish eggs slid around my back and tall grass gashed my arms and legs. There was life and death there in that swamp—birth and decay. The red-winged blackbirds perched on the cattails and watched me with apparent disdain. Dragonflies dived and buzzed at my head. Tadpoles and minnows tickled me as they swam about. The mud and goo that oozed between my toes was like heaven itself. I loved it there, immersed in the juice and slime of it, stinking to high heaven. That was the good life to me."

Now, at 50, Linda still feels the need to swim in that swamp. "I've proven I can function well in the world. Now it's time to return to the swamp. I want more experiences like that, that make my hair stand on end.

"From 50, I can see time better—past and future. And I can get in touch with the small speck I am and feel both the importance and unimportance of my life.

"I don't know who I want to 'be' next. I feel like I'm on a path. I made a big shift last year. I thought through what I'd do if I got down-sized or fired. I asked every possible question of myself and others. It freed me up and gave me a sense of peace. I feel I can accept anything that comes along now—meet it and even greet it.

"When I turned 50, I had no idea I'd get so much pleasure out of my own imagination—my own private world. That's been the greatest joy of my life. I always thought the good life was attached to achievements or adventure. But now I realize that the good life is being in the swamp, feeling everything deeply."

Great breakthroughs result from a single moment in which a person lets go of his or her usual assumptions and looks at things from a new point of view. Creating the good life is a similar process. Life can never be adequately discussed or conceptualized, but only created by living in our own questions, by continually unpacking and repacking our bags.

The Zen master, Suzuki, said, "I'm an artist at living, and my work of art is my life."

People who are "artists at living" are bold enough to question the status quo—to accept that someone else's truth could be a lie for them. They are also willing to recognize when their own truths have become a dead end, in which case they demonstrate the courage to let go. They accept what they can from an experience and move on.

People do not always make breakthroughs by refusing to quit. Sometimes they make them because they know when to quit. When they realize that enough is enough, that old patterns aren't serving them, that it's time to repack their bags.

## Packing and Repacking

As we negotiate the ages and stages of our lives, we continually give up parts of ourselves. We unpack, and discover new parts. We repack.

People like Linda, with the courage to "test their edges" eventually break through to greater aliveness and fulfillment. People who "stay packed" out of fear or unwillingness to let go gain only a false sense of security. By covering up, wearing masks, and shutting down, they eventually experience a death—the death of self-respect.

Unfortunately, very few of us have anything in our development that provides us with the knowledge and skills to unpack and repack our bags. The self-awareness required to know *what* to pack and the discipline needed to realize what to *leave behind* typically come totally as a result of trial and error. With little skill, even less direction, how is it possible for us to know how much to carry? It's no wonder that so many people are burning out from carrying too much. To succeed now and in the 21st century, we must learn to unpack and repack our bags often. To do this, we must ask the right questions.

These "quest-ions" are the trail markers on our quest. They may not always point us in the right direction, but if we ask them and seek their answers with energy and creativity, they will help keep us moving forward.

Here's another postcard exercise that may help you keep moving forward. And help you get a better sense of what the good life is for you.

# Postcard Exercise

## The Good Life

1. Sit quietly in a comfortable chair at a time when you will have a half hour or so of solitude. Take a look at your life. What is good about it? What is missing? What does it feel like right now? Take a look at all of it. Is this what you want? What is happening at work? How are your relationships? How do you relate to where you live? How are you expressing your talents? Consider what is satisfying and what is not in your life. Where are you putting most of your time and energy? What life or work decisions would you make if you suspended thinking about money?

2. Having engaged in the above reflection, you're now ready to complete your postcard. Taking into account all that you've thought about, come up with a snapshot representation of what the good life is to you. Again, it can be a photo, a sketch, a slogan, an ink blot—whatever. Put that image on the front of your Good Life Postcard. (Make a photocopy of the postcard form on page 114, or use an index card, or an appropriately-sized piece of paper.)

3. On the back of the postcard, describe your image of the good life in a short paragraph, or single sentence if possible. Keep in mind the formula: *Living in the place I belong, with the people I love, doing the right work, on purpose.*

4. Send your Good Life Postcard to an appropriate Dialogue Partner. Preferably, this will be someone who you've included in your vision of the good life. Wait for them to respond, or if you don't hear from them in about a week or so, call up and see what they think.

# Unpacking Your Bags

# CHAPTER 3

# What Am I Carrying?

For every parcel I stoop down to seize,
I lose some other off my arms and knees,
And the whole pile is slipping, bottles, buns,
Extremes too hard to comprehend at once,
Yet nothing I should care to leave behind.
With all I have to hold with, hand and mind
And heart, if need be, I will do my best
To keep their building balanced at my breast.
I crouch down to prevent them as they fall;
Then sit down in the middle of them all.
I had to drop the armful in the road
And try to stack them in a better load.
— ROBERT FROST, "THE ARMFUL"

## Unpacking Your Bags: Choices, Choices, Choices

Ever had the airlines lose your luggage?

You know that laminated card they show you with all the suitcase styles? Ever wonder why there are so many different types of baggage? And so many options for packing things away? Ever wonder what type of person carries this style or that? Or what your own bags say about you?

Go into any luggage store. You'll find briefcases, duffel bags, knapsacks, overnight bags, suitcases with wheels, suitcases with built-in carriers, suitcases with carriers that come off. Fabric choices galore—vinyl, nylon, leather, aluminum, burnished steel, horsehide, alligator, lizard and snake. You can get big, bigger, biggest, small, smaller, and smallest, all the way down to tiny little bags that only hold a toothbrush. Whatever you want, wherever you're going, however you're traveling, there's a special bag just for that purpose. When it comes to choosing baggage for a particular journey, the choices are endless.

Of course, the same is true—to a far greater degree—in our journey through life. Unfortunately, most of us make our choices quite early on. We come out of school and trade in our bookbag for a brand-new briefcase. We make our choices based on what we see around us and what our needs are at the time. But many people end up carrying this same bag the rest of their lives—long after it's outlived its usefulness.

In this chapter, we'll help you take a look at what you're carrying. Does it still fit? Has it gotten a little worn around the edges? Is it time to think about visiting your internal luggage store for something new?

The big question is: Are the bags that you're carrying still the right ones for where you are going for the rest of your life?

## The More, the Merrier?

As you begin the process of unpacking and repacking your bags, you'll discover a simple truth that you may already know: You always start out with too much—although you don't know it's too much at the time.

Dave tells a story to illustrate:

When I prepared to hitchhike across Canada, at the age of eighteen, I thought I had my life pared down to the absolute minimum. Everything I owned fit into my backpack . . . almost. I needed more room for the real essentials: my set of wood flutes, the I-Ching, a brass lockbox that held my identification cards and address book, my journal, my special pen for journal writing, the pouch in which I carried my stash when I had any, my favorite hash pipe, camera, extra glasses and sunglasses, and the packet of letters from the woman for whose love I was taking this journey in the first place. So I strapped a daypack to the top of the backpack frame, creating a hybrid carrying system that towered over me like a swooping vampire.

Thirty miles north of Toronto by the side of Canadian Highway 1, I tipped over and couldn't get up. As I struggled to release myself from the belts and buckles that secured my carrying system to me, a pickup truck pulled over and the elderly farmer behind the wheel offered me a ride. He and his younger passenger, who I soon learned was his son, had a good laugh while I fumbled about, separating my two packs in order to lift them into the back of the truck. They were nice enough though, to let me ride in the cab with them, which turned out to be a godsend, because we hadn't gone five miles before the skies opened up and it began to rain torrentially. Unfortunately, it was still pouring when they dropped me off at a roadside rest area half an hour later. I splashed around to the back of the truck and dragged out my backpack. The farmer began to pull away. By the time I noticed, he was twenty yards gone and accelerating—and with him my daypack!

I sprinted down the exit ramp after him, waving my arms and screaming like a crazy person. If someone had been watching, I'm sure they would have taken me for the proverbial ax-wielding hitchhiker, but that didn't stop me. All that mattered at that instant was my most prized possessions were speeding away from me. The rest of my gear, left soaking in a huge puddle, could have been washed away for all I cared.

As luck would have it, the farmer had to slow for traffic and I managed to catch up just as he was about to merge onto the highway. He saw my face in his side window and burst out laughing. No doubt I looked hysterical—and I was. My vocabulary had been reduced to two words: "Wait!" and "Stop!" but I was getting a lot of mileage out of them, repeating each word in a steady stream at the top of my lungs.

While the farmer and his son slapped their thighs and wiped away tears of laughter, I scrambled back into the rear of the truck and recovered my daypack. I hugged it to my chest with all my might as if I could squeeze away the terror I'd just experienced. Clutching it close like a favorite teddy bear, I plodded back down the ramp towards the rest of my stuff. I'm sorry to say that I didn't even turn to thank them for the ride.

Subsequently, it has occurred to me that the experience was a pretty good example of how I have too often operated. I've weighed myself down with so much stuff that I haven't been able to enjoy the trip I'm on. Instead of taking care of myself, I spend all my energy taking care of my stuff. And then I pay so much attention to the heavy part of my load, I neglect life's treasures, which then of course, tend to disappear into the distance. Only if I'm really lucky—or scream really loud—do I have any chance of my ever seeing them again.

## The "Packing Principle"

The Peter Principle seems to be at work when it comes to stuff—whether that stuff fills a knapsack or a lifestyle, whether it's freeze-dried food packages or important responsibilities at work. The Peter Principle says that people in an organization rise to their level of incompetence—they keep getting promoted until they end up in a job they can't do effectively.

Most of us in our lives accumulate by the same principle.

We keep adding things and responsibilities until we get to the point that we can't manage them anymore.

It's the "Packing Principle."

What then, is the solution? There are two parts to it. First, decide how much you're really willing to carry. And second, decide what goes and what stays.

Ultimately, it comes down to a series of trade-offs. What are you willing to trade in one area of your life to get what you want in another? The unpacking process is a matter of reviewing what you have and considering each item in light of the trade-offs you have to make to keep it. Some of the trade-offs our interviewees have shared with us include:

- Freedom vs. security
- Higher salary vs. less responsibility
- Things vs. time
- Comfort vs. growth
- Home vs. office
- Self-expression vs. social approval
- Making an impact vs. leaving no trace
- Knowing where you are vs. getting lost

Repacking becomes a matter of finding the right balance between the important priorities in your life. The first step is to examine what you're carrying, and see if it appropriately reflects the trade-offs you are willing to make.

## Unpacking: The 3 Bags of Life

If you imagine your life as a journey, then you can think of its various components in terms of the various bags you are carrying. We like to say that everyone carries three different bags. These are:

1. A Briefcase—your Work baggage

2. An Overnight Bag—your Love baggage

3. A Trunk—your Place baggage

To really unpack, you need to open each one and examine its contents. The best way to do this is in a dialogue with someone else—preferably the person most likely to be affected by any decisions or choices you make.

On the pages that follow, you'll find questions designed to help motivate those dialogues. We encourage you to use them all, and develop your own, as you unpack. Have your partner ask you the questions and take notes as you answer. Do the same for him or her. Or record your dialogue on tape for review afterwards. If you can't locate a Dialogue Partner, that's okay. You can ask yourself the questions in a "dialogue" with yourself. Just be sure to give yourself ample time to respond.

## "What Do You Do?"—Unpacking Your Briefcase

- What are your hidden talents? How does your work give you the opportunity to express those talents?

- What do you think "needs doing" in today's world? How does your work allow you to make a contribution to that?

- What is your ideal work environment? How does your current work environment compare?

- Who do you want to serve in your work? How does your current work involve you with those people?

- Picture your typical work day. What is it filled with? How much of "you" goes through the door and how much of "you" do you check at the entrance?

- Imagine your ideal work associates. How do your current work associates stack up?

- Does your work make you happy?

# "Who Do You Love?"—Unpacking Your Overnight Bag

- Who are the people you feel closest to in your life and why?

- What do you miss most when the people you care about most are away?

- What life dreams do you share with the people you're closest to?

- Describe a typical day spent with those you love best. What's the best part of the day?

- How did you meet those you're closest to? What drew you to them first?

- Do you spend as much time as you like with your loved ones? How could you spend more?

- How do you want to be remembered by those you love?

- Does your relationship life make you happy?

# "Is There No Place Like Home?"—Unpacking Your Trunk

- When you think of "home," what image springs to mind?

- What are the qualities that make "home" home to you?

- What is your "most prized possession"? If your house was burning down, what would you grab?

- When you look around your home, what makes you happy? What feels like clutter?

- What about your sense of community? Do you feel like you belong? How are you contributing?

- If you could live anywhere, where would it be? Why aren't you living there now?

- Does your home and living environment make you happy?

# Unpacking Your Bags: The Trip Checklist

As you go through the 3 Bags of Life, what you're doing is creating a *Trip Checklist.* You've seen these at camping or luggage stores, or maybe you're the kind of person who creates them on your own. It's simply a way to make sure that you're bringing all you need with you on your journey, while at the same time, not bringing too much. It's a way to avoid the "Packing Principle."

You're taking stock of where you are and how you've gotten here. You're examining the choices you've made in your life and trying to determine if the decisions still serve you. You're seeing if you still have the answers. Or if even the questions have changed.

The *Trip Checklist* isn't a test. Think of it more as a resource for planning. There are no right or wrong answers. The point is to simply answer as truthfully as possible and learn as much about yourself as you possibly can.

Use the *Trip Checklist* on the following page to take a look at the next phase of your life. See if you're carrying these items, or if some of the other things you're lugging along are taking up too much room.

# The Trip Checklist Dialogue

Having completed the *Trip Checklist* you may be asking yourself, "What direction am I really headed in, anyway?"

The checklist provides you with a structure for discussing your direction in life with others. It's another opportunity to engage in dialogue, which is an important part of the checklist. Use the checklist in a discussion with a Dialogue Partner to ask:

- How is your current trip going?

- What are your hopes and dreams for the next leg of your journey?

- Where are you now and where do you hope to go?

# The Trip Checklist: 12 Essentials for Unpacking

| Checklist Item | Have It | Need It |
|---|:---:|:---:|
| **Passport** | ☐ | ☐ |
| Sense of Purpose—a reason for the trip. | | |
| **Adventuring Spirit** | ☐ | ☐ |
| Willingness to let my spirit roam, to plan my own itinerary. | | |
| **Map** | ☐ | ☐ |
| Sense of direction to my journey. | | |
| **Tickets** | ☐ | ☐ |
| Talents or credentials to explore new places and opportunities. | | |
| **Traveler's Checks** | ☐ | ☐ |
| Enough money to enjoy the trip. | | |
| **Travel Partners** | ☐ | ☐ |
| People to share the experience with. | | |
| **Travel Guides** | ☐ | ☐ |
| Key sources for advice along the way. | | |
| **Luggage** | ☐ | ☐ |
| Appropriate style and size of bags for the trip I am on. | | |
| **Carry-on Bag** Stuff I need at hand to make the trip enjoyable— books, learning tools, and a sense of humor. | ☐ | ☐ |
| **Toilet Kit** | ☐ | ☐ |
| Energy and vitality to enjoy the trip. | | |
| **Travel Journal** | ☐ | ☐ |
| Travel tips and key "lessons learned" from past trips. | | |
| **Address Book** | ☐ | ☐ |
| Contacts with important people in my life. | | |

- What type of bag (backpack, attaché case, duffel bag, etc.) best illustrates where you are and where you're going next?

- Who are you traveling with and how does it feel?

Keep the dialogue open and alive by a willingness to share as deeply as feels comfortable. Remember, this is about *unpacking* and *repacking*. The more fully you can *unpack* your innermost thoughts and feelings, the more vital your discussions will be. At the same time, there's no need to turn your dialogues into therapy sessions. They should be fun—or at least not too painful. Like your life, they should be filled with all the stuff you need, and free from all the stuff you don't.

## How Much Stuff Is Enough?

Each of our lives is, in fact, a short trip. In the grand scheme of things, we're penciled in for a very brief journey. On the other hand, this is all we've got. So it's no surprise that many of us go through life weighed down by the importance of it all, crushed beneath our load of literal and figurative baggage.

You can gain insight into how to lighten your load by imagining yourself setting out on a journey into the wilderness. If your pack is too heavy, it means you're too attached to the life you are leaving behind. If it's too light, it means you may not have enough to stay alive. The question becomes, How much is enough?? The weight of your pack ultimately determines the quality of your trip.

Because the more we have, the more we have to carry, entering the next phase of our trip requires lightening our load—not just physically but also emotionally. Like trekkers on safari, we inevitably have to ask, "What do I really need to carry?"

In the middle stages of a trek, people often become fatigued because they're carrying too much. They lose their sense of joy because they're weighed down by all their stuff. They experience a version of the distinction that comedian George Carlin draws so eloquently between our "stuff" and other people's "stuff." In his routine, "A Place for My Stuff," our own stuff is "stuff," while other people's stuff is "shit." During a trek, people often come to believe that their own stuff is shit, too.

This also happens to many of us during the middle stages of life. It starts to feel like an all-or-nothing choice. We get buried in responsibilities and attachments and want to either chuck it all or just give up. Often, this is what's behind the traditional mid-life crisis that sports car dealers know so well.

On treks in Africa, most people don't have a problem knowing what to carry. Their problem is knowing what to leave behind.

The trick is to find the balance between what to carry and what to leave so that you have all you need, but need all you have.

In the movie, *The Jerk*, Steve Martin plays an idiot who, through pure dumb luck, strikes it rich by inventing a special handle for eyeglasses. He becomes phenomenally wealthy and indulges himself with a brand-new mansion full of consumer goods. Soon of course, his life goes down the tubes—his personal relationships fall apart, his self-esteem crumbles, and finally, in a classic scene, he staggers through his house, getting ready to leave for good, boasting that he doesn't need anybody or anything. But he can't completely let go. He picks up a chair, an article of clothing, a vacuum cleaner.

"I don't need anything!" he bellows. "Except this. . . and this. . . and this. . ."

By the time he walks out the front door of his home, he's draped in all kinds of things, with furniture and appliances hanging off every limb. And because it's Steve Martin, he's also got his pants around his ankles.

It's like this for most of us (except for the pants). We approach the process thinking, "I don't need nothin'," but before we know it, we're groaning beneath the weight of all the things we can't live without. Here then, is a postcard exercise to get you thinking about the one—and only—thing you really, really, really need. Sharing this with a Dialogue Partner will also help you test out whether what you think you need really is what you do.

# Postcard Exercise

## The One Thing I Really, Really <u>Really</u> Need

1. Go through your home, mentally or physically, until you've come up with the one thing you really, really, *really* need. For example, if there was a fire, what item would you grab first? Keep in mind that the "one thing" doesn't necessarily have to be a valuable possession. It might be a treasured photograph, an unpublished novel you're working on, or even your favorite coffee cup.

2. Using whatever medium you want, create an image of the "one thing" and place it on the front of the postcard. (Make a photocopy of the postcard form from page 114, or use an index card or appropriately-sized piece of paper.)

3. Write a brief explanation about why this one thing is the "one thing" and send it to your Dialogue Partner. Wait for your partner to respond, or if you don't hear from them in about a week or so, call up and see what they think.

# CHAPTER 4

# Why the #@&%! Am I Carrying It?

*"Not I, not anyone else, can travel that road for you.*
*You must travel it for yourself."*
— WALT WHITMAN

## The Weight of Silence

Many people feel crushed by the load they themselves have accumulated. They feel smothered by responsibilities, financial commitments, and work demands, they've willingly taken on. But they tell us that now, they can't possibly unpack their bags because other people are depending on them to carry the load. But nine times out of ten, when we ask them if they've discussed their feelings with their loved ones, they tell us they haven't!

As it turns out, many people are carrying more than they like for reasons that don't *really* exist. They've simply never asked their families, friends, or partners for permission to lighten their load. More importantly, they've never asked themselves.

In this chapter then, we'll help you do so. You've already considered *what* you're carrying. Now it's time to ask yourself "Why the #@&%! Am I Carrying It?"

# Carrying On About Carrying

Dick tells a story to illustrate the importance of asking yourself the "Why the #@&%! Am I Carrying It?" question:

> I got caught in the rain in Toronto recently and ducked into a bookstore. While I waited for a break in the downpour, I wandered into the self improvement section. As I stood there dripping into my already soggy running shoes, I was instantly reminded just how much weight people are carrying and how desperately they want to lighten their loads by "becoming joyous," or "following their bliss," or "living the life they were meant to lead."
>
> After searching the "L's" to comfort myself that the "world's largest bookstore" (as they claimed to be) carried my books, I landed in the "M's" and pulled an old friend off the shelf, *The Courage to Create*, by Rollo May. I opened it at random, and this paragraph leapt off the page at me:
>
> > If you do not express your own original ideas, if you do not listen to your own being, you will have betrayed yourself. Also, you will have betrayed our community in failing to make your contribution to the whole.
>
> May reminded me why I'm doing what I'm doing, why I was up in Toronto getting caught in a downpour, and helped inspire the ongoing effort to keep making my contribution with this book.

Obviously, people vary tremendously in their expression. Artists and poets often set the standard for the rest of us. Their courage to create can be an inspiration to us common folk for whom just finding another reason to fight the rat race one more day is often, in itself, an act of great creativity.

Making a contribution is what it's all about. We all want to feel useful—that we're using our talents in the service of something we believe in and that we're honestly making a difference to its success. When we feel that sense of usefulness, that sense of attachment to something larger than ourselves, we feel an almost boundless sense of energy. We know exactly why we're carrying what we're carrying, and feel strong enough to carry even more.

In Minneapolis, there is a community theater company called The Heart of the Beast Mask and Puppet Theater. Every year they stage a huge parade and festival to celebrate May Day. The whole community is invited to participate. For weeks beforehand, the theater is filled with people of all ages building papier maché floats, masks, and costumes. The energy in the room is incredible. Inner-city kids work side by side with suburban grandparents. Everyone is focused on the task at hand—busy as can be—having a great time. Laughter fills the air. The most common phrase you hear is "What can I do to help?"

It becomes apparent to you—when all is said and done—that the opportunity to help is something all of us are looking for. We want to work on something we believe in, work hard on it, and see our own hand in the result.

Of course, this doesn't always happen in our jobs. Many people feel that their efforts make little, if any, difference. And besides, what's the difference, since who cares about what they're working on, anyway? People lose their sense of direction and energy because they don't know why they're doing what they're doing. Work becomes a habit, a mindless progression from one day to the next.

The same thing happens in our relationships. We get to the point where we're doing things by rote, without even thinking about why we're doing them. We just repeat the patterns—patterns no one is really happy with—without ever stopping to ask why.

Dave recalls this story:

A couple summers ago, I was working really hard on a variety of projects, and never was able to find time to take a vacation. Finally, though, near the end of the season—Labor Day Weekend, actually—I carved out a day off. I was really looking forward to spending a day with my wife, Jennifer, and having our summer vacation, short though it would be.

We set out about 9:00 A.M. and headed out of the Twin Cities toward Wisconsin, where we were certain we could find a small resort within three hours or so to stay overnight. After three and a half hours of fighting vacation traffic, we came to our first possibility, but it wasn't "just right." (This was our entire summer vacation, after all, and we wanted the place to be perfect.) So we decided, because it was only about an hour further, to drive up all the way to Lake Superior, which we'd never seen before.

There was a detour and it took us more than two hours to get to the lake. It was as big and beautiful as advertised, but there wasn't a hotel room anywhere. So, we resolved to drive a bit more and see if we could find something. Another two hours later, all we'd seen were "no vacancy" signs, and the prospects for lodging didn't look good. But I was ready to keep going. This was our summer vacation and we were going to have it, no matter what it took. I gritted my teeth and stomped on the accelerator.

That's when Jennifer asked me why I was so intent on finding a place. Why did I want to keep driving? Why was I doing this and getting myself so worked up about it? I said I thought she was the one who really wanted to keep looking. She answered that all she really wanted was to spend some time with me—it didn't really matter to her where we did that. She suggested what, in fact, had been going through my head at that very minute, but which I had been afraid to propose: why didn't we just turn the car around and drive back to the Twin Cities? We'd be there in time to have dinner at our favorite restaurant and could sleep late the next morning in our own bed.

So that's what we did. Five hours later, for a grand total of almost twelve hours in the car, we pulled into the restaurant four blocks from our house. We knew it was totally nuts, but unlike our wanderings earlier in the day, we knew exactly why we were doing it. And it made for one of the best—or at least most memorable—summer vacations we've ever had.

As ridiculous as Dave's summer vacation was, it's less ridiculous than what happens to us if we don't ask the question Jennifer asked, "Why are we doing this?" If we don't ask, we don't know. And if we don't know, we can't change—or even continue doing what we're doing with a renewed sense of purpose. The question applies to every component of the good life:

- Why am I doing this work?
- Why am I involved in this relationship?
- Why do I live where I do?
- Why do I consider this my purpose?

The answers aren't easy, and just thinking about them isn't enough to change things. But at least thinking about them is a step, one everyone who wants to lighten their load needs to take.

## Four Reasons for Carrying

When you get right down to it, there are only four reasons why you might be carrying what you're carrying. You can break this down into two scales and create a matrix to help identify where you stand. One scale is a continuum between current enjoyment and future payoff. We either do something because we enjoy it, or because we expect to get something down the road. The other scale is a continuum between self and others. We either do something for ourselves, or we do it to help or assist others.

Combining these yields the four categories. So you might be carrying what you're carrying because:

- You enjoy it now for the pleasure it gives you.
- You enjoy it now for the pleasure it gives others.
- You are willing to put up with it now for something it will provide you with in the future.
- You are willing to put up with it now for something it will provide others with in the future.

An example of the first category might be a job, hobby, or pastime you really love doing. For instance, you may have no problem getting up on a cold winter morning at 6:00 A.M. to go skiing.

In the second category might be hosting a party. It might be tons of work for you, but you enjoy it because it's fun for people you care about.

A good example of the third category is physical exercise. You may hate your aerobics class or detest swimming laps, but you do it because you know that afterwards, you'll feel better for having done so.

Into the fourth category falls a lot of people's work. You may not be crazy about your job—you may not even like it at all—but you do it because you have a family to support, or because you want to someday pay for your children's education.

Obviously, in all four of these categories, there's some overlap. For example, you may enjoy some aspects of your job while putting up with others because they may eventually lead to something else. The point is not to go through your life and pigeonhole everything you do into one or another category. It's simply to help you see that the answer to the question, "Why the #@&%! am I carrying it?" is not that complicated. You can, with a little introspection, develop a pretty clear sense of why you're doing what you're doing and why you're carrying what you're carrying.

More importantly, this prepares you for doing something about it. It sets you up to either lighten your load or steel yourself for the burdens you've chosen, because there are really only two things you can do: You can either keep carrying or stop carrying.

What most of us do, though, is vacillate. Or whine. If we feel that something's weighing us down—a relationship, a job, the burdens of home ownership—we're usually not willing to just let it go. At the same time, we're often unable to accept the burden as a choice and change our attitude about it. We don't take the time to do what Dick did with the items in his knapsack: decide if we really want to be carrying them, and if the answer is "yes," to carry them as happily as possible.

Human beings have a remarkable ability to persevere. History is filled with stories of men and women who bore incredible hardships in the name of a cause or concern they believed in. On the other hand, most of us have a hard time flossing regularly because it hardly seems worth the trouble.

When we unpack and repack, a good deal of what we want to do is simply decide what's worth the trouble. And then, having decided that something is worth it, own it—take responsibility for that choice—and bear the burden (if it still feels like one) with as much good humor as we can.

Here then, are some tips that may help you do so with more of a smile. (We've related them to items on the *Trip Checklist*, but you can apply the tips however you like.)

- *Share the weight* (Travel Partners)
  If you're feeling particularly weighed down by responsibilities or commitments, ask for help from family members and friends. You'll probably be surprised by how willing your loved ones are to lend a hand. And impressed by how much real assistance they can offer.

- *Let go of one thing* (Luggage)
  Sometimes we forget the weight we're carrying is cumulative—that it's a collection of many things. So we're apt to see our burdens as an all-or-nothing choice—either we have to grin and bear all of it or drop

everything and run. In reality, though, our choices are broader. We can let go of one or two things without completely throwing in the towel. Try giving up one responsibility at a time until you've reached a place that feels more manageable. Maybe you don't have to quit your job. Maybe you can just turn down a volunteer opportunity or two.

- *Shift the load* (Travel Journal)
  The day-to-day grind wears us all down. Doing the same thing day after day after day makes even lesser burdens weigh heavily in the long run. So try shifting the load if you can. Take one day a week and go into work later—even if you have to stay later in the evening. Alter your routine. Shift things around—same as you would if you were carrying a physical load.

- *Remember why you're carrying this* (Passport)
  If you feel inordinately weighed down by things, it may be that you've forgotten why you're doing what you're doing. Sometimes tapping back into your reasons for carrying on will give you the strength to do so. And if not, it may be that the burden isn't something you actually want to put up with, anyway.

- *Give yourself a destination* (Map)
  It's a lot easier to put up with a difficult job, a stormy relationship, or a place with which you're unhappy if you know it's not forever. So if you're feeling crushed, give yourself a destination—a few months, half a year, whatever seems appropriate. If things don't improve within the time limit you've set for yourself, then it's time to make the necessary changes. But until then, at least you know there's a possible end in sight.

- *Ask for directions* (Travel Guides)
  Hard as it sometimes is to admit, few of us are true pioneers. Just about anything any of us is going through

has already been gone through by someone else. The good news is, we can ask directions of these people. They can give us tips on how to travel more lightly, and how to navigate through difficult terrain. Friends, partners, co-workers, older family members are all available as guides. We just have to ask.

- *Organize your itinerary* (Adventuring Spirit)
Sometimes things just seem like too much because we don't really have a handle on all there is to do. Doubts about our responsibilities nag at us, making them seem twice as heavy as they really are. Sometimes the solution to this is simply to get better organized. Make some lists. See exactly what it is we have to do, and by when we have to do it. Sometimes writing things down makes the anxiety associated with them disappear. At the very least, it gives us a checklist to keep track of everything we think we ought to take care of.

- *Locate yourself globally* (Address Book)
Perspective is an amazing thing. You may feel like you've got the weight of the world on your shoulders, but when you compare yourself to other people in the world (or even other people you know), it might not seem so bad. This isn't to say that your burdens aren't real, but rather to remind you that you may not be tapping the deepest reserves available. You, like other people around the world, may be a lot stronger than you think.

- *Trade places* (Tickets)
Our friend Doug Thomas was sick of being a full-time businessperson. His wife, Laura Cooper, was fed up with staying home all day with their pre-school children. They solved both their problems when they figured out a way to switch places. Laura went back to the bank she'd worked at before having children, and Doug quit

his full-time job to devote himself to freelance writing and taking care of the kids during the day. Laura and Doug had to make some serious adjustments in their schedules and scale back their lifestyle somewhat but ultimately, this was well worth it for both of them. Doug's only regret was that he had waited so long to ask Laura about making the change. "I could have been doing this a year ago," he said, "if only I'd had the courage to seriously consider it."

- *Take a rest* (Toilet Kit)
  There's nothing like exhaustion to make us feel really exhausted. But there's nothing like a rest to help us recharge. So if you're feeling particularly overloaded, try to find a way to take a break. A short vacation, an afternoon off, even a mid-day nap can work wonders.

- *Remember that you're a tourist* (Carry-On Bag)
  New Yorkers live their entire life in Manhattan and never once take the ferry to see the Statue of Liberty. Real Parisians wouldn't deign to visit the Eiffel Tower. It makes a great cocktail-party story, but is this really any way to live? Isn't it also the point to experience as much as we can? How do we know we don't like green eggs and ham until we've tasted them? So, if you can, sample whatever experiences are available to you. Approach them with a spirit of adventure. Perhaps many will turn out to be silly, boring, or simply a waste of time. But how will you know until you try?

- *Indulge yourself* (Traveler's Checks)
  Generosity of spirit doesn't require that you spend money like water or treat yourself to every new delight that becomes available. But at the same time, if you're constantly denying yourself, then you're not experiencing the full array of possibilities, either. So, it's not a bad idea to occasionally indulge yourself by treating

yourself to something you really want. It doesn't have to be a new car or trip around the world—sometimes a pair of in-line skates you've been coveting or a weekend in a different city can make all the difference.

## The Weight of Success

The more we do, the more responsibilities we have, the heavier our loads tend to be—and the more important it is that we ask ourselves why we're carrying what we're carrying. And yet, it is precisely when we need most to ask ourselves this question that we find it most difficult. We're too busy, too weighed down by success to stop and reflect.

All around us, though, help is available. We don't avail ourselves of it. Side by side on the bookstore shelves, row after row, are books that encourage us to introspect about the meaning of our journey through life. To scratch even the surface of the wisdom contained in these volumes, a person would have to retreat from the world to study full time. The only way we could ever possibly get these messages about life would be to withdraw from life. But life is full of riddles that can only be solved by living them. As Kierkegaard said, "Life can only be understood backwards, but it must be lived forwards."

Ironically, the most important issues in our lives—*work, love, place, and purpose*—are also usually the most difficult to deal with. And the problems with which we need the most help are the hardest for us to ask for help with.

As Dick notes:

> The clients who grace my office all carry bags of varying weights. Most are successful people, but they feel burdened. Often, their work or their relationships do not make them feel that they are living the good life. They want to spend their precious time doing something that has meaning both in its performance and its product. Many

feel impelled to make a mid-life career change, hoping to find more in their work than mere financial rewards.

Even my most successful clients are asking questions. The rat race is taking its toll on them in the form of stress, anxiety, depression, drug and alcohol abuse, and divorce. They feel isolated and unable to ask for help. Most do not readily seek help for their problem. They are not fond of self-improvement courses or books. They're uncomfortable talking about their problems with people in their organization. So, they seek me out privately to talk—to lighten the load.

Usually, it has taken a "wake-up call" of one sort or another to get them thinking about their problems. And unfortunately, due to the effects of the wake-up call, they're often much less able to deal effectively with their problems than they would be normally.

The evidence is pretty persuasive that most of us—even the most successful of us—will go through periodic wake-up calls when we feel as if we are carrying the weight of the world on our shoulders. As Rollo May put it in *The Courage to Create*, "Emergence is often experienced by the individual as emergency with all its attendant stress." In other words, wake-up calls wake us up.

Dick talks about his own series of wake-up calls.

Several years ago, I was a journeyman adult. I had come into my own. I was confident. I was settled. I was successful, comfortable in my way of life. Surprisingly to me, it skidded to a halt. A series of *wake-up* calls shifted my mental furniture around and permanently rearranged it. A second parent died. I divorced. A work partner died. My son left for college. My world caved in. I had to tunnel out.

My father was only 68, and we'd never had a chance to say good-bye to each other. Everyone told me that he did not suffer. There wasn't any time. The emergency crew and the doctor who happened to be nearby agreed. He'd been struck by a catastrophic physical event—a massive coronary—while walking in the skyways of downtown St. Paul. Death was instant and final.

My father disappeared, taking with him my past and his future. I was struck by the feeling that by dying so young, he had aged me overnight. A new person crawled out, weighted down with the heavy bags of sadness. I decided I had to repack for my own future.

Eleven years later, my mother at age 78 died in my arms. We did have a chance to say good-bye to each other. With her death, the generational curtain flung open, completely. I no longer had any protection from the raw edge of total responsibility for my life. Unpacking and repacking was not a choice.

After her death, I looked in the mirror. I saw a mid-life adolescent, in some ways no different from what I was at 18. Confused, frightened, yet amazed and excited by my life with the same sense of longing for distant places, the same wild curiosities and romantic yearnings. I remember having those same exact feelings when I was 18. The years between 18 and 49 seem like moments, not decades.

## Saying Good-bye to Others, Hello to Yourself

Everyone says good-bye to someone or something at various times in his or her own life. It's usually not easy, but the letting go of things is a natural part of life. In order to keep moving forward, we have to occasionally leave things behind. We have to move on. In order to grow, we have to deal with losses, whatever they are—death of a loved one, job layoff, divorce, loss of property, loss of a dream, launching children. Journaling, introspection, and most importantly, dialogue, are how we handle the losses. They're how we allow the newfound lightness of our load to keep from weighing us down.

If we don't let others know how we feel, then we continue to carry the weight alone. Just when we should be letting go, we're burdening ourselves even more. When Dick's daughter Greta went away to college, he wrote to her from his "empty nest." The thoughts and feelings he shared were an essential part of the letting go process:

Dear Greta,

And so it has come down to this—you're leaving. Really leaving.

You say, "I'm not really leaving, Dad. I'll be back." Yes, you'll be back. It isn't as if we won't see each other again. We'll talk by phone weekly for awhile. But when you return you'll come as an adult. By day-to-day standards, you are gone for good. It's amazing to realize that all those "empty nest" clichés are real. "Enjoy them now—they're gone quicker than a wink of the eye."

Now I tell other parents in my seminars the same thing. I lecture them to "seize the day," to realize that this phase of their lives will be over in the wink of an eye. And they smile and pretend to understand.

You're at an age where you "want to do your own thing," don't want to be told about things—want to experience them for yourself. Much as you don't want to hear it or even to think about it, the reality is you can't understand me just now. You will. If you have children, you will understand the mixed joy and loneliness of ending 19 years of living under the same roof. You'll understand the depth of love a parent has for their child, which so few words adequately express. As you remember your years at home with me, you may think of the frustrations of school, sports, and relationships. My years recall the summers at the cabin, Hawaii living, Colorado and the daily connections of listening conversation.

You can roll your eyes and wonder how adults can be

so weird. I once felt the same. Yet, now, like a typical counselor, I try to convince you to "seize the day"—that life is indeed short, like the wink of an eye. It is a feeling that rolls off my tongue easily and then evaporates in the air. I have indeed let go even though I have longed to hang on. One of your and my favorite songwriters, Harry Chapin, tried to tell us about this moment in his song, *Cat's in the Cradle*, which deals with a young boy growing up admiring his father, and saying he's "going to be like him." The father is busy and on the run, never really spending the time he promises the boy. Life moves on, the son grows and becomes busy. The father ages and becomes less busy. He has grown up like Dad. The chorus you know so well is, "When you comin' home son? I don't know when but we'll get together then. You know we'll have a good time then."

I played that song last night and was moved by it, and I cried. I never knew how true the song was until now.

When you coming home Greta, I don't know when, but we'll get together then. You know we'll have a good time then. 'Til then . . .

Love,

Dad

## Risking New Ground

It takes courage to look at what we're carrying—and even more to consider leaving some behind. It's much easier to just live with what we have, secretly longing, complaining out loud.

All our lives we wait to grow up, and then suddenly we discover that we are the person that *adult* things happen to. Who among us predicted that discouragement would be part of the package? Many of us feel like Ernest Hemingway did shortly after his forty-third birthday, when he wrote, "I would be happy to fish and shoot, and let somebody else tug the ball for a while."

At mid-life, it often feels like our lives have doubled back to the starting point. The same questions that we wrestled with earlier in our lives return to haunt us. At mid-life, we're adolescents all over again, standing just outside a new place in our lives, feeling that strange adolescent mix of self-assurance and abandonment, certain that we have all the answers, but suspecting that the questions have suddenly changed.

Like teenagers, we feel the heavy weight of life's responsibility and that same ambivalence about whether to shoulder them or not. But at mid-life, we possess advantages that we lacked at eighteen. For one thing, we don't have to create ourselves from scratch. Or do we?

Adult development experts from Carl Jung to Daniel Levinson have written of the importance of mid-life. The "afternoon of life" was the phrase that Jung used for the time when we can see back to what we were and forward to what we may become. Levinson spoke of "full-fledged adulthood" when we can rejoice in our individuality and our humanity. We can arrive at the place we started from and know it for the first time.

In the movie, *Dead Poets' Society*, Robin Williams plays professor John Keating, who has returned to the prep school he attended as a youngster to try to introduce the young men of the school to the joys of English literature, and more importantly, to life. Throughout the film, as they struggle with self-discovery, he challenges them to let their true voices speak.

At one point, he leaps up on his desk and asks, "Why do I stand here?" He answers his own question: "I stand on my desk to remind myself that we must constantly force ourselves to look at things differently. The world looks different from up here. If you don't believe it, stand up here and try it. All of you. Take turns.

"If you're sure about something," he says, "force yourself to think about it another way, even if you know it's wrong or silly.

When you read, don't consider only what the author thinks, but take time to consider what you think . . . Risk walking new ground."

To *risk walking new ground* is a challenge we face constantly throughout our lives, and never more poignantly than at mid-life. Almost everybody harbors a desire to be something other than what they have become. Nearly everyone feels compelled to examine his or her own life and ask, "Why am I carrying all this?"

Our interviews, experience, and involvement with people at mid-life have led us to believe that nothing is more important to fulfillment in the second half of life than the willingness to "risk walking new ground."

Our culture has traditionally taught us that shouldering the same load no matter what the circumstances is more honorable than unpacking our bags and letting go. We hang in there because we are conditioned to believe that we are failures if our relationships or jobs end. In fact, it may be just the opposite. Making that discovery is what repacking is all about.

## Getting Here From There

Repacking is a cradle-to-grave process. It's something we need to go through again and again in our lives to sustain a feeling of aliveness no matter what our age. The good life isn't something we can get and keep—it's a process of continually reinventing what it means to live in the place we belong with the people we love, doing the right work, on purpose.

We can, however, at any time, design our lives so as to be living our vision of the good life at that time. The key to this is a conscious awareness of what we're carrying and why we're carrying it. One person who has managed to develop the reinventing awareness—and fairly early in life—is Dick's son, Andrew Leider. Even as he began taking his first few steps into adulthood, Andrew decided to try to live his vision of the good life, rather than find himself years later dreaming of or having regrets about what he never did when he had the chance.

At 23, Andrew is living in the right place—Red Lodge, Montana—with people he loves, doing the right work—he is an Outward Bound instructor—on purpose. Friends and former college roommates envy the choices he's made. He says: "They tell me, 'I wish I were doing something like you're doing, but I couldn't take the time. I saw an opportunity and felt I just had to take it in this job market.' "

Andrew compares their situations to his own—a situation he's designed—by regularly asking himself, "Why am I carrying this?"

"Most of my friends are driven by their current visions of the good life, just like I am," he says. "But they're already strapped to cars, apartments, furniture, and loans. Within the next five years, most will probably be married, have kids, and be well on their way, while I'll probably still be traveling in the mountains. If you're driven to a 5th Avenue lifestyle, then you won't be happy until you get there. I'm simply not there.

"For now, 'right work' is what I'm doing. I love the process of working with others as a team to affect people's lives. I like working on hard questions. With Outward Bound, I definitely feel a part of something important. People work here for a common purpose. We share a lot of the same values. We all seem to like doing things in unique ways. I guess that's why we all enjoy experiential learning. The purpose and values of that learning are more important than where it takes place . . . as long as it's outdoors.

"Minneapolis is the place I know best, where I grew up. But home now, I feel I can create wherever I am. I'm not settled yet. I live in four separate worlds—my family, my few college friends I have chosen to stay connected with, my Red Lodge local friends, and my extended Outward Bound family. Home is not one place. It's the way I feel wherever I happen to be. I'm trying to put as much joy into wherever I am, and with whatever I currently have."

Andrew sums up his vision of the good life this way: "My needs are pretty minimal. I don't have financial desires . . . yet! I have what I want—time and good work. I can get by with very little. It costs to live; it costs to get sick; it costs some to do the things I love to do outdoors. I want to keep enough in savings so I can take care of myself and still have time. That's the good life to me now."

*What is the good life to you, now?*

Is your vision as clear as Andrew's? Do you know what you're carrying and why you're carrying it? Or is it time to think some more about unpacking and repacking?

## Unpacking Dialogue Questions

In its major forms, unpacking can be one of the most painful of human experiences. At the same time it can be intensely liberating. How about you? What are you carrying? Are you in a major period of questioning whether to let go of a relationship or job?

Think of a particular situation you're struggling with. Decide whether it falls under the heading of work, love, place, or purpose. With that specific situation in mind, reflect on the following questions and prepare to have a dialogue with your partner about them.

- Can I really expect the situation to be any better somewhere else? Or with someone else? How?

- Is what bothers me about this job or person something I would have only with this job or person?

- What would it take to "unpack my bags" and stay here committed?

- At what point have I thought enough about my situation? At what point is "hanging in there" a mistake?

- If I "repack my bags," am I willing to experience . . .
  —Temporary criticism?
  —Temporary loss of friends, family?

—Temporary loss of place?
—Temporary loss of income?
—Feeling that I'm selfish?
—Feeling that I let go too soon?

To make it easier to engage in that dialogue, here's another post-card exercise that may help.

# Postcard Exercise

## The One Thing I Really, Really, <u>Really</u> Don't Need

Unpacking involves looking at both the good and bad in your life—the ugly, too. As you unpack, you'll probably be shocked by some of the baggage with which you're weighed down. There may not exactly be skeletons in your closets, but chances are, there will be at least a few things that have seen better days.

For instance, an artist we know, who after about 20 years of struggle, had finally gotten to a place in her life where nearly all her work was showing in galleries and selling, still carried around an attitude that made her question the validity of everything she was doing at almost every opportunity. Frankly, it was just a habit—and a habit that wasn't serving her. When one of us pointed out to her that for the last five years, all of her work had been met with great critical and commercial acclaim, it was like a light was suddenly turned on. Not that she changed her attitude right there, but she did begin to recognize that the old pattern was just that—an old pattern. By learning to let it go, she was able to find a real sense of ownership about all she had accomplished. But the first step was still to let go of what she didn't need—the one thing she really, really, *really* didn't need.

1. Go through your life, mentally or physically, until you've come up with the one thing you really, really, *really* don't need. What's the one thing that's weighing you down most heavily?

2. Using whatever medium you want, create an image of the "one thing" and place it on the postcard. (You know what to use for the card.)

3. Write a brief explanation about why this one thing is the "one thing" and send it to your Dialogue Partner.

4. Wait for your partner to respond, or if you haven't heard anything in about a week or so, call up and see what they think. Use the unpacking dialogue questions above to keep the dialogue as vibrant and compelling as possible.

# Work Bags

CHAPTER 5

# What Do I Want To Be When I Grow Up?

*"What is the good of life if its chief element, and that which must always be its chief element, is odious? No, the only true economy is to arrange so that your daily labor shall be itself a joy."*
— EDWARD CARPENTER

## How Will I Do My Living?

Because our only possession is our life, or rather our living, our most fundamental question is, "How will I do my living?"

Do you wonder if there is a better work life for you? Are you wasting your natural talents because your career chose you, rather than you choosing it carefully? Do you need more time for personal growth? Is your work in balance with your family and personal needs? Do you long for a sense of fulfillment in your work?

The quest for "how will I do my living?" is a lifelong journey, but one which people don't take until they're ready—not one moment sooner. Being ready usually means feeling a level of pain or frustration for which repacking is the remedy.

At mid-life, most of us are finally ready. It's a time of transition. We find ourselves in that in-between state in life, leaving behind an outgrown but still perfectly serviceable past, and moving toward a future that resists all efforts to bring it into clear focus. As we contemplate what's ahead, we feel a strange combination of disorientation and excitement.

Gazing back on our lives is more than just sifting through memories. It also involves poring over images of what the good life has meant to us at various points along the way. We recall the good times and wonder how many more of them there will be. We review our accomplishments in our careers and wonder if our best work is behind us.

Whether consciously or unconsciously, what we often long for most is some way of extricating ourselves from who we've been. We need some way to break out of the boxes we have built for ourselves. To break free of the inertia that holds us to a self-image that needs to be cast off, like the nautilus moving into a new chamber. The same natural process that causes the nautilus to leave old chambers leads human beings to enter new ones as well.

At times, we all wonder if we're alone in our doubts and questioning. And yet we're reticent to share our doubts and questions with others. Most of us actually have what turns out to be a secret longing to be more adventurous—a longing that we rarely admit to. Sadly, what happens is that we end up letting other people take our adventures for us. We let "professional explorers" on the Discovery Channel have the real experience of which we partake only vicariously. But it doesn't have to be this way.

Adventuring in the outer world, and just as importantly, *inventuring* (adventuring in the inner world) is possible for all of us throughout our lives. In fact, if we allow ourselves to, we can make it the focus of our life's work.

The big question when we were children was, "What do you want to be when you grow up?" It was too early, perhaps, to ask, "What sort of life do you want to be living when you grow up?" As sociologist Max Weber put it, the modern dilemma is, "Do we work to live or live to work?"

Most of us will admit that mostly we have lived to work.

We've drawn a distinction between what we have to do and what we want to do. But if we're lucky, we can one day get to the point where we discover that distinction is specious. When we're really adventuring and inventuring, what we want to do and what we have to do merge. The difficulty, though, is in letting go of all the have-to's and want-to's we've accumulated earlier in life.

Ultimately, what we are searching for is that sense of internal rhythm that explorers feel on their most exciting journeys. It's that feeling of internal and external connectedness—knowing where you're going, but not knowing how to get there. It's a combination of romanticism and practicality.

Living and working the good life means being a "practical romantic." We have to deal with making a living, paying college tuitions, loving our partner, doing good work. We have to pay mortgages and orthodontist bills. Thus, we have to continually ask, "How will I do my living?" To that extent we have to be practical.

But we also have to be romantic. We have to love. We have to be in love with people, places, and purpose. We have to be willing to engage in the utterly romantic and ultimately absurd quest to live the good life. Even though the path it leads us on wanders all over the place

Life, though, was not meant to be linear. The path from birth to death is not a straight-line journey. It's a zig-zag. A loop-the-loop. A switch-backed trail broken up by much retracing of steps. Our society, however, typically tries to reject this. And the result is the horrifying prospect of ending up successfully retired, at the end of a linear life.

The linear point of view says first get an education, then work hard, then retire so you can finally begin living. But by that time, many people have forgotten how to live, or else they're so exhausted by getting where they've gotten that there's no life left.

The alternative is to live all your life as fully as possible. To challenge the existing script. To wander as opposed to sticking to the straight and narrow. Of course, this is scary. It's not easy. It means we have to continually ask questions about our life, our love, our work.

On the other hand, there's no escaping it. Sooner or later in every life there comes a time when established patterns around which we have organized our lives come apart. We come to question our assumptions about nearly everything. The patterns that have gotten us to where we are begin to feel more like heavy weights than reliable guides. We begin the struggle to "let go"— unpack and repack our bags. We feel like children all over again, and find ourselves asking once more, "What do I want to be when I grow up?"

The truthful answer isn't as simple as it once was. Work has many "truths" for each of us. Since childhood, most of us have thought about what work means, and we constantly scrutinize our assumptions and reframe them as we come of age. Just as love has different meanings at different stages of life, work too takes on new meanings along the way.

Here are three truths that we think are true about work. It seems to us that these truths influence and even define how most people do their living.

## Work Truth #1:
## People Don't Choose Their "Calling," It Chooses Them

Life is not long enough to try everything to discover our right livelihood. Where we grew up, when we grew up, and our vocational family tree all influenced our work choices. How did you choose your work? Here are some answers we've heard:

- I considered a number of options seriously, explored each one, then picked one. Choosing my work was a difficult decision.

- At an early age I decided what I wanted to do and never considered much else seriously. Choosing my work was easy.

- I didn't have a clue about what I wanted to do; I just took what was available and things developed from there in a way that's kept me satisfied enough.

- I was forced to take whatever job I could find and I just stayed in that field. Through circumstances, my work chose me.

- The decision was more someone else's than mine. It was just expected that I'd enter a certain line of work and I did. I've never committed myself to it, though I'm good at it.

Work satisfaction has a lot to do with how it was chosen. The key ingredient is how consciously and with how much autonomy we've made the choice.

Because most of us don't know who we want to be when we grow up, we must get experience under our belts to be sure of our calling. But by the time we get that experience, some of us feel it's too late to make a choice, so we ignore the calling or just refuse to listen. As a result, there are many more people who are never sure of their calling than those who are sure.

During the first half of our lives, someone else usually writes our career script. At mid-life we are challenged to co-write, edit, or toss the original script.

We are dynamic, not static. We grow and our needs change. False starts or productive mistakes give us a "practice field" to learn what work we most enjoy doing, our calling.

Vocation comes from the Latin *vocare*, to call, and means the work a person is called to from the deepest part of their being.

But the quest for a true calling must be renewed and deepened throughout our lives. Joseph Campbell captured the essence. "The call rings up the curtain, always, on a mystery of transfiguration. The familiar life horizon has been outgrown; the old concepts, ideals and emotional patterns no longer fit; the time for passing the threshold is at hand."

This is often what is happening when we seek mid-life

career changes. We are not just switching jobs—we are pursuing our calling. And this requires crossing a threshold into a deeper part of ourselves.

# Work Truth #2:
# People Are More Sure of What They <u>Don't</u> Love To Do Than What They <u>Do</u> Love To Do

Ask many people what their talents are and how they enjoy expressing them, and they'll tell you they don't know. But ask them what they don't like and what they can't do, and you'll get a list a yard long. Experience has educated them in the negatives, but done little to inform them about the positives. This makes sense, actually. In order to truly dislike something, we have to experience it.

Try this out. Consider what are the two or three worst jobs you've ever had. What did you like least about them? What kind of people did you work with? What did you learn about what *not* to do in the future?

Hopefully, the jobs that you hated most came earlier in your career. When we're first starting out, we often have to take jobs we don't like—just to make ends meet. We're forced to try a lot of jobs that we wouldn't otherwise think of.

For most of us, when we're younger, the problem isn't just that we don't know what we like—we also don't know what we're good at. We haven't identified our talents. Or even if we have, we haven't developed confidence in them. Or ourselves. Belief in yourself comes from the knowledge that you have the talents to be what you want to be.

Talents are a source of energy within each of us that are always waiting to be discovered (or rediscovered) and expressed. Tarthong Tulku, a lama from Eastern Tibet, speaks of this in his book *Skillful Means*. "By using skillful means to enrich our lives and bring our creative potential into everything we do, we can penetrate to the heart of our true nature. We then gain an understanding of the basic purpose in life, and appreciate the job of making good use of our precious time and energy."

This knowledge of what we call *doing the right work*, together with a strong sense of talents and purpose in life, is an essential part of answering the question, "What do I want to be when I grow up?"

In their classic *Living the Good Life*, Helen and Scott Nearing propose that the "objective of economic effort is not money, but livelihood." They explain that the purpose of working is not to "make money" or "get rich," but rather to secure an existence that is harmonious with one's deepest beliefs and most powerful feelings. In 1954 when their book was first published, they noted they knew of few people who shared their attitude, and that this was the source of much of the hardship—economic as well as emotional—that they observed. No doubt the numbers are no greater today, and the hardship no less.

A high percentage of people who truly feel that they are living the good life, have work that uses their talents as opposed to a job they do mainly to earn money. Think about this: Whose work more often inspires our deep admiration? That of the mid-level corporate executive who earns six figures for manipulating theoretical concepts, or that of the simple craftsperson who transforms raw material into useful beauty?

What is it about the craftsperson's livelihood that so appeals to us? First, most genuinely seem to enjoy their work. They are immersed in it. Go to the house of someone who makes guitars for a living, and you'll probably see fretboards and tuning pegs all over the place.

Second, most craftspeople work at jobs that come naturally to them—work that uses their unique talents. In her book, *Do What You Love, The Money Will Follow* Marsha Sinetar writes, "It is as if they instinctively know what they must do with their time and energy and then determine to do only that."

Once there was no distinction between art and craft. In

medieval society, painters and sculptors as well as potters and weavers were members of craft guilds. A person "was" a painter or a carpenter—their work, their way of life, was central to their identity. They saw their livelihood as a means of centering their existence in order to discover and link with their divine source. "Craft" simply meant making beautiful things for use, a task the craftspeople saw as a tribute to the craft itself, their communities, and ultimately, their God.

Craftspeople didn't see themselves as doing the work solely by themselves. It was a shared effort, with shared results. Members of the craft guild did not sign their work, and if they worked alone, it was for the convenience of the task, not personal credit. Craftspeople worked with no pride in accomplishment, but with a joy in *accomplishing*—quite a bit different from today where the focus is usually on product, with little, if any, attention paid to the process. So it's not so surprising that these days, more and more people are looking for work that meets more than mere financial needs. They are searching for a livelihood that feeds the inner hunger—the hunger to express their talents.

Walter Kerr, in *The Decline of Pleasure*, writes, "If I were required to put it into a single sentence my own explanation of the state of our hearts, heads and nerves, I would do it this way: We are vaguely wretched because we are leading half-lives, half-hearted, and with only one-half of our minds actively engaged in making contact with the universe about us."

To say that many people feel half alive at work is probably an understatement. In our interviews, a much more common complaint is that they feel "half dead." People are secretly asleep. They sleepwalk through their days, half-heartedly using half their minds, but at the same time, they're terrified that they're wasting potentially half of their one and only life.

Each of us wants to feel unique. And what most of us mean by that is we hope to discover some innate specialness which is our birthright, which no one else has in quite the same way. Ironically, most of us are so scared to be different that we hide our uniqueness any time it rears its ugly head. So we're hungry to discover and express our talents because we need to be reassured of our uniqueness. We all want to feel that we're not just another grain of sand on the beach but that we've been put here for some unique purpose.

When it comes to acknowledging or owning our talents, most of us are terminally blind. We're taught not to brag or extol our virtues. Richard Bach notes in his book, *Illusions*, "Argue for your limitations and sure enough they're yours!"

Everyone has some excellence seeking expression. Everyone has talents of which they are unaware or which they downplay. Uncovering those talents involves a learning process which has steps to it, much like the process by which one learns to ride a bike or to swim. Each step has to be mastered before the next step can be approached. But like riding a bike, once you've got it mastered, you never forget!

You'll discover your talents by examining:

- Things you can't remember learning but somehow know how to do.
- Things you do superbly with little effort.
- Things that others observe your skill in more readily than you do.
- Things that you learn rapidly and that you enjoy learning more about.

And of course the best way is to ask close friends, family members, and colleagues.

"What are my talents?"

Take the label off. "You're a good lawyer" is not a description of your talents. Ask them to describe you instead in terms of what you're good at. "You're a superb listener!" is much better.

The more clearly you've identified your talents, the more easily you'll be able to tell if your work really suits you. If your job only engages a fourth of your favorite skills, you're probably working with only a fourth of your enthusiasm. Enthusiasm is from the Greek *entheos*—to be "called" by God. So it's no surprise that people whose ears are closed to their calling have little enthusiasm for what they do.

## Work Truth #3: Life/Work Repacking is an Absolute Survival Skill Today

The idea of a permanent job is obsolete. Your job, today, is never safe! The work world is in constant turmoil. Once-powerful businesses teeter on the brink of extinction. Companies whose names used to be synonymous with security are laying people off in record numbers. Your job may disappear out from under you at any moment without warning. These days, nearly everyone will be "between jobs" at some time.

It doesn't even matter how good a job you're doing. Excellence is no defense. You solve problems creatively? You consistently add value? These are no longer defenses against searing competition, rapid technological change, and relentless restructuring.

You must be prepared to go job hunting for the rest of your life. No one owes you a job—not your present employer, not your union, not even if you work for Mom and Dad. It's up to you to create your future. In the 21st century, almost everyone up through the highest ranks of professionals will feel increased pressure to package themselves as a marketable "portfolio" of talents.

As the paradigm of work shifts from making a product to providing a service, work itself is being redefined. We're seeing an increased need for learning and higher-order thinking, and at the same time, more scrambling for footing in shifting organizations.

All of us will be rethinking, reinventing, and repacking the structure of our work. Many of us will end up working for a "network" of organizations linked to customers and suppliers via technology. If you've been keeping up with your reading, you'll recognize this model as the "virtual organization"—a place pared down to its core competencies and sending out for everything else—including lunch! In the future, the key question for most people will not be, "Where are you on the corporate ladder?" but "What do you know how to do?" So it's time to ask yourself that same question. *What do you know how to do?*

Too many of us define ourselves these days by our "tools." When someone asks us what we do, we say, "Oh, I work with computers." Or, "I run a printing press." Even highly-trained professionals define themselves like this: "I'm a radiologist. Or "I drive a truck." The problem is all those tools are going to be obsolete in a few years. So if you've built a career based on your tools, you'll be out of luck. And out of work, too. Instead of getting known for your tools, you need to build a reputation based on your portable talents.

*What are your "portable talents"?*

Regardless of where you work these days—at a large corporation, a small business, or at a computer in your basement—the message is the same. You are on your own. You have to see yourself as a business. You have to consider yourself your own corporation, *You, Inc.,* and like any corporation, be ready to develop a comprehensive strategic plan for growth.

If we can recycle bottles, cans, and newspapers, we can certainly "recycle" ourselves. To prosper in this volatile world of work, we must be ready to recycle ourselves. In other words, to repack our bags.

And even if this weren't the case, even if the workaday world was as stable and predictable as in years gone by, there's an even more important reason why life and work repacking is a critical survival skill: *Most of us tire of our work once we have mastered it.*

Feeling burnt out? Rusted out? Bored? Maybe you've reached the end of the road on your current job. All jobs have "lives," cycles of learning, mastery, plateauing, and declining. Because we have brains, we require new stimulation for growth, food for the mind, body, and soul. Some people try to ignore this. Others create life crises on purpose. A friend of ours claims, "Three years is enough for anyone in one job path. After that it's a repeat performance. The fun challenges will have been met and creativity expressed. Your curiosity fades, productivity flattens and numbness settles in!"

George Brett ended his baseball career recently. After 20 record-breaking seasons, the desire waned. He said, "I wasn't that excited when I did something good. I wasn't getting that down when I did something bad. I wasn't that happy when we won. I didn't feel as bad when we lost. There's something about riding a roller coaster. If you ride a roller coaster 162 times, you're ready for something different."

## Having Your Mid-Life Crisis on Purpose

The mid-life crisis, which we prefer to call the "mid-life inventure," presents us with an opportunity to reexamine our lives and to ask the sometimes frightening, always liberating questions, "What do I want?" "What do I feel? "What must I do now to feel right with myself?" "What are my dreams for myself and what fears have blocked me?"

In a career counseling practice over the last two decades that has been predominately composed of people in mid-life, Dick has seen the pattern again and again. The "mid-life inventure" represents a turn within, a wonderful, though often painful, opportunity to redesign ourselves.

The Gospel according to Thomas states, "If you bring forth what is within you, what you bring forth will save you. If you do not bring forth what is within you, what you do not bring forth will destroy you."

Many people are designing new workstyles, bringing forth new views of the good life, new definitions of success. Success has different meanings at different ages and stages of life.

Tom DuFresne, a successful real estate developer, who, in his forties, sold his company to go into the business of creating educational materials for high school students, said, "What matters to me now are relationships and experiences. When I was younger, I had a passion about acquiring things. Creating a successful lifestyle. Now, success to me means successful relationships and passing things like this down to my kids."

On the whole though, we are a society of notoriously numb people—lonely, bored, dependent people who are happy only when we have killed the time we are trying so hard to save. We worry constantly about making a living, but rarely about making a life. In our businesses and financial markets across the country, people scramble frantically trying to make a killing, but end up instead killing their lives.

The vast majority of people endure their jobs because they see no other way to make a living. In addition, their work organizes, creates routine, and structures their lives. At the very least, most jobs force us into a rhythm of weekend leisure, Monday blues, Wednesday "Humpdays," Friday T.G.I.F., and regular paychecks. Our minds and bodies become so attuned to these rhythms that they become part of our own internal clocks. We forget that there are other ways to spend time or save it to do the things and be with the people we love. We forget that there are other pathways that lead out of the wilderness, away from the rat race.

## A Path Through the Wilderness

Psychologists know that the capacity for growth depends on one's ability to internalize and to take responsibility. If we only see our life as a dilemma that others have created, a problem to be "solved," then no change will occur. If we have a failure of nerve or are lacking in courage, no repacking can occur.

Conversely, if we view life as a product of our own imagination as a mystery to be discovered, then we tend to remain flexible and open to new input all the time. If we're willing to take risks and face new challenges, we can continually recreate ourselves to meet the changing circumstances of our ever-unfolding experience. The invitation of the "mid-life inventure" is to become aware (unpack our bags), accept responsibility (repack our bags), and risk the journey of life to which we are summoned.

Daniel Boorstin in his monumental book, *The Discoverers*, documents that medieval geographers and theologians blocked the exploration of new worlds for centuries by their refusal to use the ancient term "terra incognito" to describe places on their maps where people had not been. They preferred to simply not include those places at all. They found it safer to limit the world than to face the fact that much of it was unknown.

Any adventure is also an "inventure." In order to seek out new lands and go where no one has gone before, one must first take an inward journey to the heart, the mind, and the soul.

To travel to that place we call "the good life" requires a similar inventure. We must survey territory we're searching for. Map out a route to get there. This type of planned inventure is the opposite of unconsciously acting out the patterns or paths of the past. And in this case, it's the only way we can hope to find what we're looking for.

Inventuring requires the willingness to acknowledge the "terra incognito" quality of what we do not know. Inventurers celebrate the unknown and appreciate the unknown wilderness in their own spirit. Naturalist Eliot Porter proclaimed that "in wilderness is the preservation of the world." We see mid-life inventuring as the preservation of the world within. Each of us is trying to express more fully who we are. Each of us has a unique path through the wilderness. There is something meaningful—and even holy—in our diversity. Without uncharted land, terra incognito, the process of living would lose much of its vitality and meaning. An inventuring life finds aliveness at the edges of discovery and growth. The purpose of life is, then, to grow. Some people naturally seem to live this way. Most of us have to work at it.

A middle-aged man in a recent workshop had spent several years making the transition from being laid off as the head of a staff department in a private corporation to teaching at a small liberal arts college. In that time, he went through several cycles— working on an advanced degree, taking a half-time job with a friend who was building a new business, simplifying his day-to-day financial needs.

In this workshop he talked about his future. He had tears in his eyes. "Some people when they realize they are about to die say, 'Oh, shit!' I'm not going to be one of those. I'm taking the risk now to create the second half of my life. I finally got it— there is a difference between success and fulfillment. I had success, but I wasn't fulfilled. Maybe success is getting what you want. Fulfillment, though, is wanting what you get. And I didn't end up wanting what I got!"

The feeling that this man had—the feeling of losing one's center—is familiar to anyone who has dealt with demands of external success while trying to fulfill internal values and needs. For those who try though, Kierkegaard may offer solace: "To venture causes anxiety; not to venture is to lose oneself."


## Celebrating the Explorer Within

Dick admits that "the life of inventuring is consistently reawakened in me when I visit Africa. Africa helps me understand and connect all aspects of myself. It causes me to open my eyes and see how I fit in. I am myself and everyone else too."

Every culture in one form or another celebrates the explorer who ventures, who experiences the world, confronts the unknown, and returns with the stories of their experience to enrich the community. At mid-life, the exploration process, often called the vision quest, takes on new significance because it brings us to a fundamental understanding of our true calling.

The inventure life is a life of continual repacking. Inventuring means we're willing to try on a wide variety of work options to develop a vision that reflects our true calling. This isn't an intellectual head trip. It's not spiritual pilgrimage just for the sake of it. It isn't latching on to every hip new philosophy that comes down the pike. Rather, it's a result of practice—regular, daily practice. The practice may include being in nature, meditating, praying, playing music, drawing, sculpting, traveling, or simply spending time alone. All of these are ways to open our true calling. Through such practice, we eventually realize a whole different level of aliveness. We come to feel our calling.

Oliver Wendell Holmes said, "Most people go to their graves with their music still inside them." Many people live their entire work lives and go to their graves never finding out what they wanted to be when they grew up.

## What Do You Want to Be When You Grow Up?

John Williamson was a Harvard-educated, articulate spokesman for lifelong-learning and new educational technologies. As a senior executive with Wilson Learning Corporation he mingled with the leading thinkers on change and leadership.

Dick remembers John like this:

I knew him as a friend, a colleague, and in his last eighteen months, as a client. He fought valiantly against his cancer while simultaneously envisioning his future. During that time, I often flashed back to scenes of him backpacking and interacting with the Maasai in Africa, so curious, so alive.

Just one day away from the end of his life, he talked about his impending losses. I sat by his bed, holding his hand. He laughed and wept unashamedly as he talked about our work together.

Staring out the window, struggling to see with his one remaining good eye, he said to me, "I always thought God had a plan for me to do something special in this life but I never really found out what it was. I feel as if I never really found out who I wanted to be when I grew up."

That statement penetrated my core. We wept together as he encouraged my work. "Push them to make a difference," he said, "and don't let them off the hook."

He died the next day.

John's words are a reminder to us that beyond all else is the driving need for each of us to "make a difference," to believe our lives have counted.

In our workshops, we often say: "No one on their deathbed ever said they wished they would have spent more time in the office." In the context of John's death, that statement is more poignant than ever.

By finding our calling, whatever it is, we make our contribution, however large or small, to our time. We discover, and bring to life for ourselves, what John called "God's plan."

If you remain open to the possibilities life presents, we believe you will eventually hear your calling. And if you develop the flexibility to repack for new inventures, we're confident you will be able to respond to it and follow.

# Postcard Exercise

## "What Do You Want to Be When You Grow Up?"

Many of us spend most of our work lives dealing with what we think we *have* to be. Here's an opportunity for you to create a dialogue around what you really *want* to be.

1. Imagine that you're just starting out in your work life (and guess what, you are!). Put yourself in the position of being able to decide to be anything you want. What would that be? If you could do anything, how would you do your living? On the front of the postcard, create an image of that job.

2. On the back of the card, describe three things you would have to do to make the work a reality. What education would you need? Where would you have to move to? Whose support would you have to solicit?

3. Send your postcard to a Dialogue Partner. Get together to discuss the possibility of making that dream a reality.

<br>

CHAPTER 6

# How Can I Lighten My Work Load?

*"If you cannot be free, be as free as you can."*
—EMERSON

## Work Is Not Working

Work is not working for many people today.

Work and how it is perceived is going through one major restructuring after another. Employees at all levels in organizations big and small don't know where they belong anymore. Or if they belong at all.

Certainly, people have always had problems related to their jobs. But these days, they're more intense than ever.

People who historically assumed their organizations would "look after them" are stunned when emerging work realities cost them their jobs and turn their lives upside-down. Many more people, uncertain about organizational plans, fearful of layoffs and global competition, wary of an unsettled economy, and unclear about the future, are being forced to repack their work bags.

People frequently tell us that their work, which they used to love, has become drudgery. Or that due to layoffs, they're doing twice as much as they were before, but enjoying it half as much. They say they're constantly tired, frustrated, and fed up. But they're reluctant to complain (to anyone in their organization, that is) because these days, they feel lucky just to have a job. They go on to tell us that they're sure there's something else they can do with their talents. But what? The "perfect job" is out there somewhere, but they don't know what it is or how to find it. They feel trapped in the job that they have and stuck when it comes to looking elsewhere.

We have an answer for them. It begins and ends with an examination of that mythical "perfect job."

## The Perfect Job?

Many people have settled for work that makes them mildly miserable day after day, month after month, year after year. When they feel the pangs of frustration or burnout, they attempt to bury their fear. They rationalize: "Hey, it's a living! What more can you ask for these days?" The message is that drudgery is tolerable—as long as it pays.

Our response to these people is probably exactly what they *don't* want to hear. First, we believe that all the money in the world doesn't make drudgery tolerable. And second, we're convinced that you don't have to settle for less than your dreams. It is possible to find the job you really want. Such good fortune is not just for a lucky few.

Everyone knows what the "perfect job" is. You get paid a huge sum of money to work in a lovely office all by yourself with unlimited travel to beautiful places and lots of time off. And nobody tells you what to do.

But the truth is, that kind of perfect job doesn't exist. Not if you define "perfect job" the way most people do—as one that has no bad parts to it, no "latrine work."

Every job has its good parts and its bad parts. It's hard to imagine any kind of work that would be enjoyable 100 percent of the time. Even sports heroes and movie stars have their bad days.

So, the "perfect job" isn't really about enjoyment. Instead, it's one that mirrors perfectly the person who holds it. And people do find, or invent, or create these jobs. They do it by working a process—a surprisingly simple one. It's a process that links who you are with what you do. The process involves developing a clarity about your talents, passions, and values—looking inside yourself to discover what you do best, what you're interested in, and the type of working environment that supports what you care about most. And then combining all three to develop a clear vision of the kind of work that links who you are with what you do.

When we talk with those who are energized by their work, who are truly enjoying it, we notice they are not in "perfect jobs." But, they are in situations that they have freely chosen. If and when they change career directions or retire, they eventually "choose" something again. Many do a combination of things as they reach for a quality of life that involves, as Robert Fulghum writes in *All I Really Needed To Know I Learned In Kindergarten*, "learning some and thinking some and drawing and painting and singing and dancing and playing and working every day some."

The perfect job isn't a standard of living. It's a state of mind and a state of being. In the perfect job, you're applying the talents you enjoy most to an interest you're passionate about, in an environment that fits who you are and what you value.

## Lifestyles of the Rich in Purpose

We're inspired by stories of people who seem to have the "perfect job"—whose talents, passions, and values are in alignment and who regularly feel a powerful sense of personal fulfillment. We've noticed common threads running through their stories, and have taken to calling this "lifestyle of the rich in purpose."

Here are some of the common threads of people who have lifestyles rich in purpose:

- They have a purpose larger than their own needs, wants and desires—a sense of how their lives and work fit into the larger scheme of things.

- They have an internal compass which keeps them "truing" to their purpose in life.

- They have clear boundaries around their two most precious currencies—time and money.

- They have a sense of their potential talents, the limits of which have not been fully tested.

- They have marked adaptability when faced with obstacles—they simply handle them as a natural feature of living.

- Their abundant energy is infectious. It gives them and the people around them even more.

- They have a strong spiritual core—a sense of some higher power in their lives.

- They have a feeling of lightness—a sense of being unburdened by the burdens they are carrying.

## How Can You have a Lifestyle Rich in Purpose?

Given these unpredictable economic times, few of us have the luxury to walk away from our jobs. Yet, according to the *Yankelovich Monitor*, an annual survey of consumers' values, Americans are more willing than ever to make a job change or take a pay cut in exchange for meaningful work.

Why then, aren't more of us actually doing it? Is it possible for us to create "lifestyles rich in purpose"? Of course. But it requires change. And change usually only happens for one of two reasons. Either we confront a crisis or we see for ourselves that a different way of life is more fulfilling than our present one.

We all have a core need to be engaged in meaningful pursuits and feel valued at work. In an important sense, these constitute the true value of work more than money. In *Small Is Beautiful*, E.F. Schumacher claims that work has three critical functions: "To give people a chance to utilize and develop their faculties; to enable them to overcome their ego-centeredness by joining others in common task; and to bring forth the goods and services needed for a becoming existence."

We need to look for opportunities to do all three of these in our jobs. Most of us manage pretty well with the third item—we're good at bringing forth goods and services. But most of us can do a better job of cooperating and joining in a common task. And doing so turns out to be one of the best ways we can develop and utilize our talents.

We often hear about "evolutionaries," inspiring people who seem to be designing or evolving lifestyles rich in purpose. Individuals whose lives center around their talents, passions, and values. People, who as George Bernard Shaw said, "Dream of things that never were and ask 'Why not?'"

Early on in the planning for this book, we sent out a survey to friends and business associates asking for stories of "evolutionaries"—people who were not afraid to ask "why not?" We were gratified at the quality of the responses, some of which we share in the following section.

## The "Evolutionaries"

Following are some stories of people who have discovered "lifestyles rich in purpose."

Glen Bobo, insurance industry marketing consultant, talks of Leif Bisbjerg, a friend from Denmark and a highly talented carpenter and builder: "Leif could have been a highly successful tradesman but has devoted his life to others over the past 20 years as a social worker. Living with great zest and sense of humor, he and his wife have worked in a Danish foreign aid program in Kenya over the last five years building and running a youth polytechnic center. I would like to better emulate his zest and his choice of life paths, which are less rewarding financially, but richer in purpose."

Linda DeWolf, hospital executive, names Ivor, her 85 year old artist friend of over 20 years: "He inspires me with his active, growing mind, always learning something new. He is a risk taker on a spiritual journey. What really impresses me is his positive view of life and how he can readily laugh at himself."

Tom Thiss, author and stress management expert, says: "Ruth Stricker, founder of The Marsh, a balance and fitness center, which is an extension of her efforts to heal herself from her 17 year struggle with Lupus, is becoming the first lady of mind/body integration. I admire Ruth for her relentless search for alternative holistic health remedies and making available to others what she has found helpful for herself."

Sally LeClaire, teacher and environmentalist, nominates football hall of famer, Alan Page, now a state supreme court judge and founder of the Page Education Foundation. Sally says: "I respect his values and the way he has become a healthy role model for youth of color and all youth who work to further their education. He is living out his vision of mentoring others. By becoming what he has dreamed to become, he is a model of success."

Fred Kiel, international executive development consultant, considers farmer and writer Wendell Berry to be rich in purpose: "I never met the man, but have read over half of his writings and they reflect his purpose. I would like to emulate his lifestyle in the sense that I believe he lives simply—on a small Kentucky farm and grows a good deal of his own food, yet he writes penetrating and moving essays and novels dealing with the common good of us all: our treatment of ourselves, each other, and the land."

Gloria Jennings, human resource specialist, cites Marian Wright Edelman, founder of the Children's Defense Fund: "She is a passionate advocate for the children of this country. She has worked hard to obtain the education and credentials she needed to do the things that she felt were worthy of her time. Edelman is a beautiful woman who has a purpose that is not self-centered, but will enrich our lives through our children."

Larry Christie, insurance agent, names his wife Jean, founder and director of the Southside Family Nurturing Center, which is the largest pre-school child abuse center in Minnesota. Larry says: "If I could look adversity in the eye each day as Jean does and still maintain the upbeat attitude that she does, then I would know I have grown into a fully mature person."

Rollie Larson, retired marriage counselor and author, also nominates his wife Doris: "We've been married for 46 years, and I never cease to be amazed by her. She drops everything to talk about a concern another person might have, and she listens intently with her heart. I have rarely known a person with so few ego needs. She has a deep spiritual life and faith, yet she is dogmatic about nothing. She is generally at peace with herself and is the most complete person I have ever known."

Nancy Cosgriff, former bank executive, now a leadership consultant, suggests Gloria Steinem, author, feminist activist, and speaker, as a whole and integrated person who speaks what she believes and feels: "She seems to be fearless and single minded in her cause of changing the status of women. She is brilliant, articulate, and writes well, and though controversial, is respected. She also is witty and funny."

Bernie Saunders, author and learning consultant, names John Holt, author and educator, who dedicated his personal and professional life to promoting lifelong learning: "Searching for ways to make learning more accessible and sustainable was his passion. He was willing, with understanding and compassion to challenge the status quo about what learning and education was all about. Somehow, he understood the natural everyday genius that embraced each person."

Richard "Rocky" Kimball, educational psychologist and experiential learning expert, chooses Sandy Sanborn, founder of The Nature Place near Florissant, Colorado: "For over 50 years, Sandy has been a pioneer and leader in the environmental education movement (before the term existed). He is a total believer in the need to protect the natural gifts of the planet. He still has the day-to-day capacity to experience awe and joy in watching a kid learn, hearing a hawk cry, exploring a fossil bed, and telling a joke. In his presence you feel you are in front of a whole life."

## Choosing a Lifestyle Rich in Purpose

*What is your purpose?*

Before choosing a lifestyle rich in purpose, we must first know what we want. To put it in another way, if we don't know what we want, how will we know if we've gotten it? But even before knowing *what* we want, we need to know *why* we want it. Knowing why we want something means knowing a little bit more about our purpose in life.

So what is "purpose"? Purpose is your reason for being, your answer to the question, "Why do I get up in the morning?" It is the spiritual core that helps us find the aliveness in all our day-to-day experiences. Nevertheless, for a lot of us, the purpose aspect of our lives is the hardest to understand because it can't really be measured and it's hard to see.

A purpose is not a goal. A goal is something that can be reached. A purpose is never achieved. It exists before you and lives on after you're gone. Purpose is a direction—like west. No matter how far west you go, there's still more west to travel. And like directions, a purpose helps you choose where to go along the route. Purpose is your lodestar, your personal compass of truth. It tells you, in any given moment, whether you're living your life "on purpose" or not.

You use your purpose to set your course in life. It's the quality around which you center yourself. Without a clear sense of purpose, you are at the mercy of the shifting terrain of the outside world. It's like being on a ship without a rudder somewhere in the middle of an ocean—you're lost, and out of control. Having a purpose, though, enables you to refind your direction and then direct your way there. It makes passages through life's major transitions (not to mention minor surprises) a great deal easier.

## Discovering Your Purpose

Your purpose is not something you have to invent—it's something you discover. Whether you're aware of it or not, it's already there. But when you do name it, you will know that you've "known" it all along.

Often it takes a crisis for people to discover (or rediscover) their purpose. Here are some questions, though, that can lead you to a discovery of your purpose outside of a crisis context. Not only does this tend to be a more effective way to discover your purpose, it's also likely to be quite a bit less painful.

The questions build a formula to revitalize your energy around what matters most to you. In doing so, we think you'll find it easier to make choices that lighten your load along the way.

But be patient. The discovery of purpose can take some time. When you come to "feel it," though, you'll know it was worth the wait.

1. What are your talents?
   Name all of them—this is no time for modesty. Then choose three you think are most important and write them down. Narrow down each to one or two words. "Loving, caring, teaching, listening, creating, etc." If you're blocked, ask a Dialogue Partner for suggestions.

   *Dick's example: "My three most important talents are my listening ability, my creating, and clear speaking."*

   *Dave's example: "My three most important talents are my sense of humor, my optimism, and my resourcefulness."*

2. What are you passionate about?
   What are the things you obsess about, daydream about, wish you had more time to put energy into? What needs doing in the world that you'd like to put your talents to work on? What are the main areas in which you'd like to invest your talents?

   *Dick's example: "My passion or focus is on adult development and in helping people to discover their purpose in life."*

   *Dave's example: "My passion is on helping people to communicate more effectively and in doing so, foster understanding among individuals and communities."*

3. What environment feels most natural to you?
   In what work and life situations are you most comfortable expressing your talents?

*Dick's example: "I most often express my talents and interest in casual learning settings (e.g., workshops) or traveling in nature settings with people."*

*Dave's example: "I most often express my talents in a one-on-one situation, either with another person or with myself."*

4. Now take your answers to questions 1, 2 and 3 and combine what you think are the most important elements of each to make a complete sentence. Use the following example from Dick as a guide:

> "My purpose in life is"
>
> *(answer to question 1)*:
>
> "to use my listening, my creativity, and my clear speaking."
>
> *(answer to question 2)*:
>
> "to help people discover their purpose in life"
>
> *(answer to question 3)*: "in natural environments."

*Dick says, "Over the years my purpose has evolved to one simple statement that moves me: "To help people discover and express their essence."*

It's important that you state your purpose in the present tense to ensure that it is always current. Again, you'll probably find that, in many ways, you've already been living your purpose all along. The choices you have made throughout your life have supported it. It does help, though, particularly during life changes, to have your purpose statement clearly in mind. That way the stresses make more sense and you're better able to connect the changes to new insights and healthy choices.

One last note: You may find you have several purposes—several issues you care deeply about. If you keep investigating, you'll eventually find a common thread that ties them all together. So, repeat the questions above as often as you wish to clarify your moving purpose.

# A Formula for a Lifestyle Rich in Purpose

*(Talents + Passions + Environment)* × *Vision* = **Lifestyle Rich in Purpose**

A "lifestyle rich in purpose" is the sum of:

- Your talents
  - Skills that you truly enjoy expressing
  - Abilities that come naturally, effortlessly, and spontaneously
  - Abilities you can't remember learning because you've been doing them effortlessly for so long

- Your passion
  - Problems you strongly feel need solving in the world
  - Issues in which you'd love to be more involved
  - Areas you obsess about or would like to learn more about
  - Activities which reflect deep and consistent interests

- Your preferred environment
  - The ideal work environment that would make it easiest or most comfortable for you to express your true talents and passions
  - Place and style preferences (Most people get hired, fired, promoted, demoted, or find satisfaction based on their ability to align themselves with their environment)

- Your vision
  - How do you see yourself putting it all together?
  - How do you envision the hoped-for future and how is what you're doing now getting you there?
  - What does succeeding in the next year or more look like?

Lifestyle is an idealized vision of how we see ourselves living and working. A lifestyle rich in purpose reflects a tremendous integration between who we are and what we're doing. It fits Gandhi's admonishment to "be your message." People who are on purpose like what they are doing and like where they are doing it. Their lifestyles fit their idealized image or vision of themselves. In the truest sense, they are simply being "who they are."

# The Secret of Lightening Your Load

Attempting to restore purpose and balance in their lives, many people today are seeking a harmonious balance between work and leisure, a connection to community, and a livelihood that is satisfying while supplying the basic necessities for health and well being, mental as well as physical. These seekers are trying to lighten their work loads, to spend more time with family and friends, and to savor the simple pleasures life has to offer. They speak of community involvement, of practicing environmental-friendly lifestyles. They feel the need to lighten up and live—quite simply, to get a life.

The word "light" in the word enlightened is often thought of in the sense of illumination. Enlightened people have "seen the light" or "see things in a new light." There is, however, another use of the word enlighten. That is, "a lightening of the load."

In *The White Hole In Time*, Peter Russell explains, "The heaviest burdens in this life are not our physical burdens but our mental ones. We are weighed down by our concern for the past and our worries about the future. This is the load we bear, the weariness that comes from our timefulness. To enlighten the mind is to relieve it of this load. An enlightened mind is a mind no longer weighed down by attachments; it is a mind that is free."

Dante was 35 years old and frustrated with his life when he wrote the first line of *The Inferno*, describing perhaps the first mid-life crisis in Western literature: *"Midway through life's journey I was made aware that I had strayed into a dark forest, and the right path appeared not anywhere."*

However it is described, middle age remains the key period in people's lives where they choose to lighten their loads. Many people ask themselves, "Wasn't I supposed to be somebody by now, or at least know what I want to do with my life?" Our research leads us to conclude that there are no set stages, transition points or predictable mid-life crises—that what happens to people is often the result of accident, personal experiences, financial circumstances, and the historical period in which they live. People naturally move in and out of phases of purpose and success.

What does commonly happen, however, is a more subtle acceptance of life's limitations and possibilities. One of two things seems to happen by mid-life: we achieve our dream or we do not. Either way it creates a problem. The sooner we accept the idea that life may not turn out as we originally planned, the more important the Purpose Formula becomes. Often a major life event—divorce, illness, losing a job, kids leaving home (or returning), deaths of parents, spouses, or friends—can bring about profound changes of purpose and direction. These can happen at any point in life, but they seem to mount up in the 40s and 50s.

Writer and director Norman Corwin, at the age of 82 was quoted in the beautiful and inspiring book, *The Ageless Spirit:* "I remember now that the toughest birthday I ever faced was my fortieth. It was a big symbol because it said good-bye, good-bye, good-bye to youth. But I think that when one has passed through that age it's like breaking the sound barrier."

Some of us before the age of 40 are put off by purpose. If we're asked what our "life purpose" is, we think that we're supposed to come up with an answer that enables our entire life, something like dedicating ourselves to the poor in Calcutta or solving the problems of the environment. If, however, we're asked to identify talents, or areas to which we are repeatedly drawn, or passions or interests that move us or give us pleasure, most of us can answer quite readily. What we haven't done is recognize that these talents and interests are indicators of purpose—they're compass readings.

Lifestyles rich in purpose are nothing more than acknowledging these phases and using them to organize our time and enlighten our lives. A "mid-life crisis on purpose" can be seen as the process of making those acknowledgments and doing that organizing. It's not a matter of veering off course; rather it's a time of reviewing the map that gets us where we want to go.

Many people find that their purpose evolves as their interests and experience change over time. They may follow one purpose direction until they've fully explored it, then shift to another focus. Developing new perspectives or the "wisdom that comes with age" can also trigger the discovery of a new purpose.

Making a living is one thing. Making a lifestyle rich in purpose is another. When you know your purpose, it's easier to draw time boundaries and choose real priorities. It's easier to know where you're going and how to get there. Not that it's easy to stay on purpose. In fact, the more you look at your responsibilities and commitments, the more difficult it seems to live on purpose.

So how do you do it? Start small. Choose to act on just one purposeful priority every day of your life. By doing so, you will eventually discover the "golden thread" that runs through your life, the path that leads to where you are going—your personal purpose.

In *The Power of Myth*, Joseph Campbell often refers to this as "following one's bliss":

"We are having experiences all the time which may on occasion render some sense of this, a little intuition of where your bliss is. Grab it. No one can tell you what it is going to be. You have to learn to recognize your own depth."

Are you willing to recognize your own depth? To follow your own bliss? Are you ready to discover and commit to your purpose?

# Postcard Exercise

## Lifestyle of the Rich in Purpose

Try to imagine how the Purpose Formula could affect your life. Take time, right now, to complete the formula.

1. On the front of the postcard, write the name or create an image of someone you know who is living a "lifestyle rich in purpose."

2. On the back of the card, jot down what you imagine their purpose statement to be. Use the Purpose Formula, *(Talents + Passions + Environment) × Vision*, to help you describe it.

3. Send your postcard to the person you named. If possible, get together with that person to learn more about his or her purpose.

(POSTCARD FRONT)

(POSTCARD BACK)

PLACE
STAMP
HERE

# Relationship Bags

# CHAPTER 7

# With Whom Do I Want to Travel?

*"I never found the companion that
was so companionable as solitude."*
— THOREAU

## Traveling Together

One of the challenges along the way to a successful long-term relationship with someone is making it through the "travel test." Let's say you've been seeing another person for a while and you've come to the point where you've decided to take a trip together. Discussing the event afterward with your closest friend you might say one of two things:

Either, "It was great, thank heavens. At least we can travel together."

Or, "It was a nightmare. It's over—we can't even travel together."

Traveling with someone is a great way to get to know them—or wish you hadn't. Little faults and foibles are magnified. Simple choices about where to eat, what to wear, and how to spend the evening, turn into major life decisions. If you can navigate through these decisions with your fellow traveler, you'll feel closer, more connected. If you can't, you'll want to return home on the next plane out.

It's the same thing, if not so obvious, as you journey through life with someone. Your ability to make decisions, solve problems, and in general, travel together successfully, has a lot to do with how enjoyable you'll find the trip. Fortunately—or perhaps unfortunately—most people, when the going gets tough, don't feel they can send their travel partners packing. A few feel inclined to take a hike themselves, but even this is not usually considered an option. Too often we just trudge along together with our partner, unable or unwilling to improve things, hoping in the back of our minds that something or someone better will come along and bring us the romance and adventure we feel we're missing.

If the success of a book like *The Bridges of Madison County* is any gauge, millions and millions of people are longing for a soulmate who'll sweep into their lives and sweep them away emotionally. But how many of those millions are willing to cast free their emotional moorings in order to experience the highest heights of passion? How many are willing to let themselves be fully seen by another person? How many are willing, as we put it, to fully unpack? Apparently, there are millions of us looking for such a relationship. But many of us are too afraid, or too tired, or who knows what to let other people see what we're carrying. In the end we want the overwhelming ecstasy of a once-in-many lifetimes love relationship, without the messiness and pain that goes along with creating one. This is perfectly understandable, if not very realistic.

The simple though incredibly difficult and hard to accept truth is this: In order to have an intense, meaningful, fully alive, and exciting relationship with another person, we have to be willing to unpack our bags. Unfortunately, no Prince Charmings are going to ride up and sweep us off our feet to live happily ever after. No beautiful, wealthy, Vogue magazine models are going to appear and whisk us away to their cottage on the beach.

In order to experience our fantasies, we have to create them. In order to have the kinds of friendships and love relationships we dream of, we have to be the kind of friend and lover other people dream of, as well. The first step then, is to get clear about just who we are in our relationships.

## Choosing Your Fellow Travelers

Dave says:

> When I was in junior high, I came home crying almost every day. There was this group of kids, and they used to torment me. One day, they ganged up on me in a snowball fight. The next, they'd steal my homework. Another time, they'd hold me down and take turns spitting on me.
>
> Finally, my mom asked me why I kept hanging around with them if they made me so unhappy.
>
> "Mom, I have to!" I cried. "They're my *friends!*"
>
> It wasn't until years later, when I actually met some people who liked me for who I was that I realized those junior high kids weren't really my friends. On the other hand, maybe they were, because they taught me a valuable lesson—not everyone *is* my friend. And more importantly, I don't have to hang around with people who aren't.

As you consider your own life and the people with whom you are surrounded, ask yourself "How many are my friends?" How many of them are what we call "nutritious people"?

Nutritious people are the people in our lives who genuinely "feed" our souls. Who nurture the deepest parts of us that need nurturing. They are the good listeners who truly hear what we have to say. Who reflect back to us our innermost thoughts and feelings. Who listen without judging. Whose eyes light up when they see us and whose presence lightens our load, too.

The most nutritious people are those who love us with the fewest plans for our improvement and who allow us to love them back completely. Such relationships need not involve even the slightest hint of sexual or physical intimacy. They are instead, the close relationships that make us feel "whole." The friends and family members with whom it feels we were meant to travel as we make our way forward through life.

## The Three Journeys of Intimacy

What we are looking for in our relationships with nutritious people is, quite simply, intimacy. As human beings in the late 20th century, we have a powerful hunger for meaningful connections with other people, but at the same time, an almost pathological inability to make them. Many of us don't even know what intimacy means.

Psychologist Marilyn Mason defines intimacy as "being connected and close through shared contact in a variety of activities that are informal, deep, and personal." She says that it is a process, not static, but active and recurring. In other words, intimacy is a journey.

With that in mind, we have identified three types of journeys we typically take along the road to greater intimacy with another person. These aren't necessarily sequential, nor do you have to cross each one to achieve a deeper level of intimacy.

As Marilyn Mason said, intimacy is a process. As such, it continues to evolve throughout our lives. Each of the three journeys evolves along with us. Nevertheless, you may find it useful to consider them as a means of seeing whether you are on the right road at the right time with the people in your life about whom you care—or want to care—most.

The three journeys are:

- Day Trips
- Weekend Getaways
- Lifetime Journey

As you read about each of these, make a note of where you are with your fellow travelers. Are you on the right journey with the people you want to be with? If not, why not? If so, how can you make the journey even better?

# Day Trips

Intimacy begins with a toe in the water. When we first meet someone with whom we feel a kinship, we usually approach cautiously with great anticipation, walking on eggshells. Human beings are funny this way. The more we like someone, the less we're willing to let on. Unlike our friends in the animal kingdom, who proudly display feathers or other finery to demonstrate their attractions, we often veil our best qualities when we feel an affinity—particularly an initial affinity—for someone else.

You've seen this phenomena at high school dances—you've probably participated in it yourself. The young people most attracted to each other are those least likely to get together. Teenagers find it much easier to talk to someone who's just "a friend," than someone with whom they might conceivably be romantically inclined. As adults, looking back on this, it's charming. We laugh at how silly and scared we were at the time.

But what's charming at 16 or 17 is downright depressing at 40 or 45. And yet many, if not most of us, continue to make the same mistake no matter how old we get. What's pathetic is that we make this mistake not with a stranger we spy across the dance floor but with the people in our lives we know and love best.

Think about it. How much easier is it to open up to a stranger on a plane or in a bar than to your "significant other" or close business associates? When was the last time you let someone close to you get really close to you?

Most of us treat our close relationships as if we're merely on a "day trip" with the person or persons involved. The continuation of the voyage is contingent on the success of each day. If things don't go well, we're gone—if not literally, at least from an emotional standpoint. Our bags are packed for a quick exit at the first sign of trouble.

You know what this is like. You come home from a party with your long-time partner. It's been a trying evening and you're both worn out. Somebody says something and before you know it, you're embroiled in the mother of all arguments, and accusations are flying faster than either of you can make them up. Soon, you're wondering why you ever got involved with this person in the first place, thinking how much richer and more exciting your life would be if only you were alone.

Why is it that even our deepest relationships are on such fragile ground? How come it seems that even the people we're closest to are only a step away from being on the other side of the planet? Isn't it odd that people who can talk all day long every day for months—even years on end, can be only a few ill-chosen words away from never wanting to speak to each other again?

And yet, this *is* the human condition. So if we're serious about moving forward in any significant way, this is where we've got to unpack our bags. In order to conceive at all of establishing and sustaining meaningful long-term relationships with our loved ones, we've got to begin at the beginning.

And at this beginning lies what we call the concept of a Day Trip. How do you truly travel *with* someone else for the course of one day? And how do you unpack and repack to do so?

## One Day at a Time

You know how it is when you're first getting to know someone you like. They can do no wrong. All their little quirks are charming. The way they hold a knife, their choice in music, the way they drive a car, it all seems inspired. You can't get enough of them. Eventually, as you get to know each other better, your appreciation for some of their characteristics may deepen. Knowing the story of why they cut all their meat before eating it, for example, may make you more accepting of their need to do so. On the other hand, familiarity may breed contempt.

So what has changed? Not them, but you. This means that if you want to reacquaint yourself with the person you once cared so much for, you can. Taking a Day Trip is an easy way to begin.

Similarly, if you're just getting to know someone and are uncertain about how far you want to travel with them, the Day Trip is a good place to start.

## Day Trip Itinerary

When we talk about the Day Trip, we're not just referring to a concept. We're also talking about an actual journey, complete with places to go, sites to see, things to do, and things to learn about each other along the way. The basic idea of the Day Trip is pretty straightforward. Packing for the Day Trip means considering what aspects of yourself and your partner you'd like to deal with over the course of an eight-hour day.

To develop your Day Trip itinerary, ask yourself the following questions.

1. Consider the qualities that you think are essential about you and to you on a short-term basis. What about yourself could you not live without for an eight hour Day Trip?

2. If you just met someone, what are the first three things about you that you'd like them to know?

3. What qualities would you want in someone with whom you were traveling for eight hours? What traits or characteristics complement your own? What about you is missing that someone else could fill in?

4. If you had just eight hours to spend with someone, with whom would you spend it? In what place? What would you do?

5. Create a real itinerary for your Day Trip. Consider the places you'd like to go, the issues you'd like to discuss, the things you'd like to do. Make it an "official" itinerary, with times and everything.

6. Do it! Take the Day Trip.

# Weekend Getaways

This is the journey of intimacy on which most people find themselves, even with the people to whom they are closest. The level of commitment you feel is about what you would expect in a situation where you knew you had to spend a weekend with someone. We're willing to "make nice" or "get along" over certain things, but because we tend to be operating under the assumption that "this too shall pass," we're typically unwilling to make any substantive changes in our own behavior or in the situation itself to make things better.

On a weekend trek, you have plenty of time to share ideas. Hopes, dreams, plans for the future—they all trip easily off the tongue. In 48 or 72 hours with someone, you can get to know them really well; you can talk about pretty much everything. But it's still talk. Over the course of a weekend, you can discuss your hopes and dreams, but you can't see them realized. You can make plans for the future, but you can't implement them. There's a certain theoretical or dream-like quality to all your interactions. It's like summer camp. Things can get fairly intense, but there's a built-in end point or escape hatch that makes everything just slightly unreal.

This is the essence of what we mean when we talk about "a bag by the door." Many of us—even in our closest relationships—are packed and ready to leave. We're just an unexpected phone call from a long-lost love, a chance meeting with a mysterious stranger, a winning lottery ticket away from picking up our bag and heading out. This is easily understandable and makes perfect sense given human nature. Historically, in order to survive, we've needed to be highly flexible and adaptable and readily willing to attach ourselves to the next stronger, better looking, or smarter king or queen who came along.

But does this serve us nowadays? How much richer and more fulfilling would our relationships be if we were more fully committed to them? What would it be like if the "bag by the door" were unpacked and put away?

The concept of the Weekend Getaway provides you with a means to consider this question. Because ultimately, what we pack in the "bag by the door" is the same as what we pack for the Weekend Getaway. Thus, examining the "whats" and "whys" of our Weekend Getaway bag enables us to look more clearly into what matters most to us. We get a better sense of what we couldn't live without, what means most to us, and what most clearly defines for ourselves who and what we are.

# 48 Hours

In the Eddie Murphy movie *48 Hours*, two days is plenty of time for a couple of lives to be completely turned upside-down. Over the course of the movie, both the star and his police detective companion, Nick Nolte, come to a completely new perspective on each other and ultimately themselves. There are a lot of laughs along the way, and plenty of misunderstandings (as well as a number of car crashes), but the eventual result is that both characters have a sort of epiphany in which their understanding for and appreciation of each other grows immensely. In just two days, they become, in the complete sense of the term, soul mates.

Despite their initial aversion to each other, they end up forming a real bond, one that is deep, abiding, and certain to last through a sequel or two.

The point is, if Hollywood can do it, you can, too. The Weekend Getaway concept can help you to establish, reestablish, and maintain deeper relationships with friends, family, and partners. And the good news is—unlike Eddie and Nick—you don't have to get in a car chase or a shootout with bad guys to experience it.

# Weekend Getaway Itinerary

Like the Day Trip, the Weekend Getaway is first and foremost an inward journey. Although you may want to take an actual getaway with your Weekend Getaway partner, it's not essential that you go away and sequester yourselves somewhere to experience it. Nor do you have to take two whole days to get any value from it. (Although it's rarely a bad idea to get away for a while.)

To develop your Weekend Getaway itinerary, ask yourself the following questions.

1. Write down the qualities that you think are essential about you and to you on a medium-term basis. What about yourself could you not live without for a weekend trip?

2. If you were spending 48 hours with someone, what are the first three things about you that you'd like them to know?

3. What qualities would you want someone with whom you were traveling for 48 hours to have? What traits or characteristics complement your own? What about you is missing that someone else could fill in?

4. If you had just 48 hours to spend with someone, whom would it be? In what place would it be? What would you do?

5. Create a real itinerary for your Weekend Getaway. Write down the places you'd like to go, the issues you'd like to discuss, the things you'd like to do. Make it an "official" itinerary, with times and everything.

6. Do it! Take the Weekend Getaway.

## Lifetime Journey

Whenever we read in the newspaper about a couple who are celebrating their 50th wedding anniversary, we tend to experience a mixture of both sentimentality and awe. It seems sweet that the pair have stayed together for so long, but at the same time, we're aghast that any two people could put up with each other for half a century. How have they weathered the changes? Have they managed to grow? Do they still love each other?

There's certainly plenty of room for debate about whether human beings are "meant" to form life-long bonds through marriage or other social contracts. Surely, it's not the lifestyle for everyone. But at some level, it's what we're all looking for. People want that ongoing, never-ending intimacy. We all want to live happily ever after till death do us part.

How then, is this sort of lifetime journey possible with someone else, especially given the transient nature of today's society and the quickly-changing needs and expectations of contemporary adults?

Peter Russell says that relationships are contemporary western society's "yoga." Yoga, in this case, is used in its original sense, to mean "work," especially spiritual work. Russell's point is that we can and should use our interpersonal relationships as a form of meditative yoga to improve ourselves and society.

Conceiving of our interpersonal relationships in a lifetime context may be one way to proceed. Imagine how things would be if, instead of clinging to the vague notion that somewhere out there, there was someone better for us, we were willing to unpack for an ongoing journey no matter how long or how far it might take us. Supposedly, this is the idea behind traditional marriage, but in practice, it works out only about half the time. And even in marriages that do stay together, it's often because the parties involved have totally checked out. They're living together, but are farther apart than many couples who have had the courage to face up to the differences and separate.

## A Grand Dialogue

Thus, the Lifetime Journey doesn't require that the parties involved remain in absolute proximity to one another. Successful Lifetime Journeys can be carried out by people who live miles, even continents, apart. Because the Lifetime Journey involves a change of perspective as opposed to a change of location, one needn't rush off to some distant location in order to maintain the connection. We're talking the "long-haul" here, so it's only natural that there are times when you and those with whom you are on a Lifetime Journey are not together.

Nietzsche called marriage a "grand dialogue." In order to sustain that dialogue, partners in any long-term relationship must engage in an ongoing "radical conversation." They must be willing to share their innermost thoughts and feelings in the most radical sense—facing their fears and honoring their differences together.

Too often, people end up tied together instead of moving along the same path. Their ideas about what constitutes the good life are not in alignment, so they're continually tripping over each other. Instead of supporting one another on the journey, they're just getting in each other's way.

For many people, the clearest example of Lifetime Journeys in their lives are the relationships they have with their children. Despite the many ups and downs associated with parenting, most people with kids manage to maintain a lifelong connection with their kids. But this doesn't automatically mean they're carrying on what we'd consider a *grand dialogue*. Mere proximity, without an abiding connection, isn't enough.

In some cases, the only Lifetime Journey a person experiences is the unconditional affection they feel toward a pet. In which case, it may not be for their lifetime the journey lasts, but only as long as Fluffy or Mittens or Rex is around.

## Lifetime Journey Itinerary

The itinerary for a Lifetime Journey becomes a reflection of your deepest feelings about yourself, your journey partner, and how you see your long-term connection ultimately unfolding. Generally, the itinerary for a Lifetime Journey is less strict than for the shorter trips. It's apt to be described in terms of purpose and direction as opposed to destination.

Still, it's useful to engage in the same sort of dialogue for the Lifetime Journey as you did for the other two. It's also not a bad idea to regularly repeat this exercise to see if you're still tracking along with your Lifetime Journey partners.

The question comes up again and again: *Are you still traveling together?* If so, how can you continue to do so? If not, how can you get back on track?

1. What about yourself would you most need on the journey of a lifetime? Consider the qualities that you think are essential about you and to you on a journey to last a lifetime.

2. If you were spending the rest of your life with someone, what are the three things about you that you'd like them to know?

3. What qualities would you want in someone with whom you were traveling for the rest of your life? What traits or characteristics complement your own? What about you is missing that someone else could fill in?

4. If you could spend the rest of your life with just one other person, with whom would it be? In what place would it be? What would you do?

5. Create a real itinerary for your Lifetime Journey. Write down the places you'd like to go, the issues you'd like to discuss, the things you'd like to do. Make it an "official" itinerary, with times and everything.

6. Do it! Take the Lifetime Journey

# Postcard Exercise

## Fellow Traveler

Writing and thinking about Day Trips, Weekend Getaways, and Lifetime Journeys is one thing. Taking them is another. The insight and understanding you'll gain by actually setting out together with another person will surpass anything you can possibly conceive of on your own. Capturing that insight will provide guidance for future journeys, whether they're with your current travel partner or someone else.

Here then, is a postcard exercise to help you recall some of your experiences. Use it to send a postcard to someone you love.

1. Pick one of the three journeys from earlier in this chapter. If you've had a chance to take one, or begin taking one, use your experience on it to create an image that represents that journey. If you haven't had the actual opportunity to begin traveling, take five or ten minutes to visualize what the journey would feel, taste, smell, and look like. Then create an image that captures the mood of this journey.

2. On the back of the card, describe the journey and list the three qualities you have brought along on the journey as well as the three that your fellow traveler brings along.

3. Send your postcard to that fellow traveler. Get together to talk about the importance of having that person as a fellow traveler in your journey through life.

4. Alternately, if you haven't been able to take a Lifetime Journey with someone else, take a Day Trip or a

Weekend Getaway on your own. While you're away, complete the front of the postcard, creating the image of the journey. Then, on the back of the card, write to someone you'd like as a travel partner, telling them what three things you miss about them most. When you get back home, contact them and discuss these in detail.

# CHAPTER 8

# How Can We Fully Unpack?

*"Love consists in this, that two solitudes protect
and touch and greet each other."*
— RAINER MARIA RILKE

## A Bag By the Door

In our relationships with others many of us keep a bag packed by the door. Secretly—or not so secretly—we're waiting for someone better. And should he or she appear, we're ready to go.

We've all seen it: a friend who takes his wedding ring off for out of town trips, another who complains about her husband, but never talks to him about what she feels, couples who see "separate vacations" as the solution to all their problems, real or imagined. Of course, the ironic thing is that these are the very attitudes and actions that keep people from forming the kinds of relationships for which they yearn.

One friend of ours bemoaned the fact that his wife did not have a "rich inner life" like he did. Consequently, he felt unable to really open up to her. Ironically, it was precisely his inability to open up that kept him from seeing his wife's deeper inner life. What he wanted to say most is what he feared to put into words most.

These types of cycles feed on each other. Relationships fall into patterns from which neither party seems able to escape. In the extreme, this becomes a pathological dysfunction. But for most of us, it just takes the form of habit, unspoken expectation, and slowly but surely eroded trust. The saddest thing of all is that it's usually our deepest, most powerful relationships that are hardest to change. Anyone can fully unpack their bags to a stranger on an airplane. But how many of us can open them up to a spouse, a partner, or close business associate?

Admittedly, it's not always like this, but all too often, it happens. Look around—or within—and you'll find a deep well of despair in the area of human relationships. Here's an arena in which our hopes and dreams exceed our capabilities. We've been given the ability to experience these overwhelming emotions, but not the skills to manage them. It's like we got the keys to emotional Ferraris, but no one's ever shown us how to drive. Is it any wonder so many of us crash and burn?

The things we do for love often turn out to be the very things that get in the way of our experiencing it. This is ironic because most of our actions are driven in one way or another by that vital need to connect with someone else in a deep and significant way. If you were to put every one of our motivations—to make money, become famous, conquer the world, *whatever*—into a big pot and boil them down, they'd all reveal the same essence: we want to be loved. It's trite but true. All our jumping about, all our inventing, everything from our first words to our last dying gasp has that same single motivation. So we keep packing more and more into our lives, all in a desperate attempt to get friends, families, even perfect strangers to love us. Ironically, we need to do just the opposite.

*We need to unpack.* We need to open our hearts, minds, and mouths and put into words what we're feeling. We need to share our innermost thoughts, hopes, dreams, and desires. Only by overcoming our fear of exposure can we truly be seen.

# The Transparent Self

Sidney Jourard, in his classic, *The Transparent Self*, predicted that people who love deeply would live longer. His theory was that if we revealed ourselves to each other, we would live healthier, more vital lives, with less disease.

Jourard's hypothesis has been validated by many longitudinal studies, including one Dick worked on in 1973. George Vaillant studied a large group of male Harvard alumni over the 40-plus years following their graduations from college. Part of the research was designed to determine what factors separated the healthy grads from the unhealthy ones. Who had become diseased or disabled, who had died?

Vaillant disclosed the startling findings in his book, *Adaptation to Life*. It turned out that neither diet nor exercise nor overall fitness was the critical factor. The single most important key to health and well being was self-disclosure.

Individuals in Vaillant's healthy group reported the presence in their lives of at least one "nutritious" person—someone with whom they could consistently share their thoughts and feelings openly. For some, it was their spouse, for others (even married), it was a friend or work colleague.

Rollie and Doris Larson, in their book *I Need to Have You Know Me*, stress the power of listening. They say it is impossible to over-emphasize the gnawing hunger people have to be really listened to, to be understood, to feel visible.

The most common reasons we hear for people "keeping a bag by the door" include:

- "She's just not interested in what I care about."

- "He just doesn't get it. And he's not interested in learning how."

- "She has enough troubles of her own. I don't want to be a burden."

- "He's too busy—there's no time."
- "She always tries to fix me."
- "I feel invisible around him."

Yet the Larsons, along with Sidney Jourard, claim that each of us has within us the potential for "courageous conversation"—self-disclosure—hundreds of times every day. They support, as does Vaillant, the benefits of fully unpacking our emotional bags on a regular basis.

Feelings "buried alive" rise from the grave to haunt us with illness and disease. When we keep our emotional bags packed, we lose touch with others and ourselves.

*So how do you do it? How do you fully unpack?*

That's a good question and one which by no means has an easy answer. But it's clear that if we could fully unpack with at least one person, we'd be well on our way.

All relationships with others mirror our relationship with ourselves. Developing better relationships with friends and loved ones means developing a better relationship with ourselves. In order to unpack with others, we need to start at square one—unpacking our own bags.

Gifford Pinchot, author and corporate consultant to Fortune 100 companies, knows what that's like. He knows that any and all positive change—whether for individuals or organizations—takes place from the inside out. "I tried success," he reveals, "and it didn't work. At one time, I believed that if I did something outstanding enough, I'd be accepted and loved. Now I know that's not true. Besides, there's a more direct route—if you accept yourself and let others in, it will happen."

Gifford has redefined things before. Together with his wife and partner, Libba, they coined the word and created the concept of "intrapreneuring" in their best seller of the same name. They've also started and operated four companies, led school and community reform projects, and have received numerous patents.

Gifford admits, "Traveling, consulting, and giving speeches

is weighing me down; I'm always working as an outsider. There's no real intimacy there. Sometimes I just want to take time and visit with friends and loved ones—like the Maasai elders, I don't want to carry a spear any more.

"The good life for me is when I'm working with friends on purposeful things—where work and love are highly blended.

"Being away from Libba does not make me unhappy; but there's an absence of 'real happiness.' Being home with her and working together, though, brings me enormous happiness."

Gifford and Libba are involved in the Cold Spring Community Conservancy near the Gifford Pinchot National Forest in Washington. The Conservancy is an educational project they helped found that demonstrates and practices using natural resources in sustainable ways. Ever the visionary, Gifford's quest now is to create a new sense of community. He wants to center his life around people who are "intrapreneuring" in their daily lives—taking responsibility to see that life works at all levels, not just in the workplace. Gifford says, "Cold Spring is a way of working together toward a dream. When I'm there, I feel a larger energy flowing through me. Nature is a catalyst, and of course, there are other inhabitants besides people."

He envisions himself there "writing and drawing and inventing and building things together in a nature-led community. People there share their stories, care about each other's lives, listen deeply to each other, and work together on things that matter. There, I feel connected on all levels. I'm unpacked, and it feels good."

## The Order of Who, What, and Where

Earlier, we discussed how different people tend to focus on different aspects of the good life in different ways and at different times in their lives. Some tend to be preoccupied with Work—the "what?" question. Others turn their attention to Place—the "where?" question. Still others tend to focus on Love—the "who?" question. Gifford Pinchot, for example, has shifted his focus from work first to love first.

So just because when you were in your thirties, you were highly directed along the Work path, doesn't mean there won't come a time later in life when concerns about Place or People take precedence. This awareness has a lot to do with self-acceptance and purpose. It also has a lot to do with developing and sustaining long-term, "fully-unpacked" relationships. In order to really connect with another person, you need to understand which of the three good life pathways they're currently traveling on. You need to support their unpacking and repacking in a manner that best suits their personal needs and inclinations. And you need to have the courage to let them understand your own needs and inclinations, too.

Being "fully unpacked" with another person means both of you are unpacked. If either of you still has a bag by the door, then something's not right. Most people, when they're less than completely satisfied in a relationship—whether it's a romance, a friendship, or even a business association—think that if only they could get the *other* person to reveal a little bit more about themselves, then everything would work out. In fact, the only trick—and it's not really a trick at all—to deeper, more meaningful relationships, is self-revelation. The more you can let someone else in, the more they'll open up to you as well.

This may sound a little arcane, but it's a simple fact of life. What trips people up is that often, they have no courage for self-revelation, no vocabulary for describing who they are and what they're looking for out of life. Using the order of who, what, and why is one way to go about doing this. Letting your partner know how you prefer to pack the three components of the good life can go a long way toward letting them see who you really are and what you need for emotional and spiritual satisfaction.

# Packing For Two (Or More)

Think about how you tend to order the good life components of *work, love, and place* at this point in your life. Which comes first? Second? Third?

Now consider this: how many times have difficulties in your relationships been attributable to the different ways you prefer to go about living the good life? How many times have you had conversations that go something like this:

YOU:  What do you want to do tonight?

THEM: How about we go to that new restaurant?

YOU:  I hate that place—the waiters are rude!

THEM: Who cares about the waiters, the food is great!

YOU:  Plus, it's all the way across town. I was thinking about something a little more comfortable.

THEM: Look, if you didn't want to go out, why did you even ask me?

YOU:  Forget it, let's just stay home then.

THEM: Okay fine, but I'm not cooking . . .

And so on and so on. When you're focused on the where of it all, and your partner is focused on the what, it's no surprise that you don't get anywhere together. Here are some suggestions for how to go about developing a "grand dialogue."

*Here's the easy part: the questions. Both you and your partner should answer these.*

In any given situation, which of the three components of the good life *(Work, Love, or Place)* do *you* tend to focus on first, second, third, and why? (Think of an example and write it down.)

In any given situation, which of the three components of the good life *(Work, Love, or Place)* does *your partner* tend to focus on first, second, third, and why? (Think of an example and write it down.)

*Now comes the harder part . . .*

You've got to talk about it. Share what you've written down about each other. See where your answers match, and make note of that. Discuss where they don't and try to figure out why. Use what you've written as a map for your continuing dialogue. Head for the places that look most tangled and twisty—that's where the real interesting stuff lives.

*Now comes the hardest part . . .*

Try to *do something* with the information you've uncovered together. Build on any revelations you've made. Here are some things you might try to put some of what you've learned into practice.

- *Give in.* Spend an evening together during which time you allow all your decisions to be driven by the other person's first packing preference. For example, if your partner begins with *place,* then concentrate on creating or putting yourselves in an environment that accords with their sensibilities.

- *Switch places.* Take on each other's roles for an evening or more. See how it feels to be in your partner's shoes. If it is someone who tends to be most focused on *work,* while you naturally gravitate toward *love,* try changing roles. See how it feels to turn your attention to your work above all. See how it makes your partner feel when you do.

- *Be the "PackingMeister."* Schedule two events. For each event, one or the other of you gets to be the "Packing-Meister." The PackingMeister gets to make all the decisions about what, where, and with whom the event is done. The idea, though, is not for the PackingMeister to greedily create an event that feeds his or her own preferences. Instead, the PackingMeister should make every effort to structure an event best suited to his or her partner's preferences.

- *Take a field trip*—a Day Trip or a Weekend Getaway—to learn more about your individual packing preferences. For example, if you want to investigate *place* together, spend a day together just getting to know where you live (or want to live) in ways you hadn't before. Visit a part of your town you're not familiar with. Or a part you don't know as well as you'd like. Do the same thing with your work. Invite your partner to spend a day (or at least a few hours) at your job. See how their understanding of what you do helps you unpack your bags. Or spend the entire field trip focused on your relationship. Go off somewhere together for a day or two and don't do anything other than get to know each other better.

# Postcard Exercise

## Fully Unpacking

Fully unpacking your relationship bags—disclosing yourself to others—promotes both health and happiness. We all need someone—at least one other person—with whom we can fully unpack our bags.

How open are you? Use the following postcard exercise to help you review your willingness to unpack your bags with others.

1. Who knows you deeply and understands who you really are?

2. What would you be unwilling to share with that person? What kinds of things have you been unwilling to share with anyone?

3. On the front of the postcard, draw an image or write the name of one person who really knows who you are, who truly sees you.

4. Think of the different ways this person allows you to "unpack." List them on the back of the postcard. Describe a recent interaction with this person that was particularly fulfilling.

5. Send the postcard to them. Wait a few days and then, if they don't get in touch with you first, contact them to do some mutual "unpacking."

# Finding Your Place

# CHAPTER 9

# Where in the World Is Home?

*"Here is where I should be."*
— Isak Dinesen, *Out of Africa*

## Where Should I Be?

Do you have a picture of where you should be? Where you would like to live? What are the chances of being able to do the kind of work you want to do and earn a suitable income there? How do your spouse, partner, and family feel? What are their pictures of where they should be?

Many of us have visions of where we would love to live and work. The purpose of this chapter is to help you focus your vision on where in the world is home. Where should you be? Where do you unpack?

Even if the place in which you're currently living is truly "home" for you, it's a healthy idea to develop a "Plan B"—an additional place to consider in the event that circumstances change. It's fun to break the boundaries of your current thinking and at least dream about the other possibilities. If nothing else, doing so can help you appreciate more fully what you have.

# A Sense of Place

If you were given the choice, now, to move to anywhere in the world, where would you choose to go? The mountains in Colorado? The high desert in New Mexico? The coast of Maine? Somewhere in the French Alps? The bustling center of New York City?

The late naturalist/author Sigurd Olson underscored our need for a sense of place. He claimed contact with nature is a necessary part of existence: "It is a long jump from the life of those days to the concentrated civilization of our cities and larger towns, and it is rather hopeless to believe that in the short space of a generation or two, we can completely root out of our system the love of the simple life and the primitive. It is still deeply rooted and it will be hundreds or thousands of years before we lose very much of it."

Dick has personally seen changes come over many people he has guided on wilderness trips. They go, for example, to Africa to climb a mountain like Kilimanjaro or see the great migration of animals. And they come back hooked on sunsets, silence, staring into the fire's coals late at night, sleeping beneath the stars, touching the basics again.

Most of our lives are no longer tied to the sun, the tides, or the changing seasons. We see hunger in the eyes of so many people today, a hunger for contact with the earth—a sense of roots, of place. Our sense of place is so tied up with our evolving background and traditions, it simply cannot be ignored. As Sigurd Olson goes on to write, "Wilderness . . . is a spiritual necessity, an anecdote to the high pressure of modern life, a means of regaining serenity and equilibrium."

We are rooted physiologically and psychologically to our wild past. Because of the speed of change, we haven't had time to shift gears. As a result, no matter how successful our lives, we can't seem to shake our past. Without some kind of contact with the earth and its simple rhythms, we feel a lack of roots. Literally, a lack of grounding.

## Always Going Somewhere, Never Being Anywhere

Two generations of us have grown up in the television age. It should come as no great surprise that many see the good life at its best as beautiful people in beautiful places. And what do we do when our own life doesn't match up? It's easy. We go faster. Or move. Of course, that doesn't always work in the long run. But who in today's television and computer culture has much to say about the long run?

There never seems to be enough time. We have less for ourselves and far less for each other. We are impatient with people who are reflective or who talk too slowly. We drive fast, make love fast, and expect our McDonald's hamburger in 15 seconds. A full calendar reflects our importance—time is money. Our weekends are scheduled weeks in advance. We rarely have time for real dialogue or for just "wasting time."

We're more organized but less spontaneous, less alive. We're better prepared for the future but less able to enjoy the present. We're always going somewhere, never being anywhere. Just where are we going anyway? Where is there?

When will I enjoy my friends? When will I be at home in my home? Will there ever be a time in my life to attend to my family's priorities?

Diane Herman, former marketing executive at Pillsbury, now a freelance marketing research and strategic planning consultant, remembers feeling the excitement of ideas and art and music she used to have earlier in her life. "I felt intelligent and very alive," she says, "and then I lost it. I lost my soul in my first marriage. Fortunately, I was able to repack and get back on track. But I refound my soul working in the legislature on things I felt passionate about."

Today at 46, Diane feels more integrated into the community through her involvement in arts, politics and her daughter's school. "I feel a sense of responsibility for this community. That was missing at Pillsbury. I felt guilty if I left to go to a school program. I had no time to volunteer or go to my kids' events." She recalls recently a meeting at her daughter's school to work on a newsletter. She laughs, "There were eight women sitting around that table; six had MBAs and were living in the same questions I'm struggling with! It was comforting to know I'm not alone."

When she left Pillsbury to create more time for her passions she says her biggest challenge was to craft a new definition of success. "When I was working full time, I was successful but there was nothing left inside. I felt hollow. The glitter of success was valid for me at one time. But then, it lost its luster."

We have observed in our interviews that people like Diane who are more fulfilled, have created a sense of place for themselves. They have learned to order their "private world." They understand that succeeding inside yourself is the game that needs to be mastered. They have come to understand that no external success will atone for internal failure. The ultimate "success test" is the *Integrity Test*:

*Are you keeping the small promises you make to yourself?*

Dick met Dan Peterson on one of his African safari treks several years ago. Dan was in the middle of a two-year sabbatical from his orthodontic practice near San Diego. After dental and orthodontic schools, a stint in the Air Force, and 20 years in a joint orthodontic practice he said, "I felt I needed to do something different. I was dying from the inside out. My partner and I had created our ideal master plan where we each worked for 6 months and then took 6 months off. It worked great for 18 years. I had it all except for one thing—inner peace. So I left."

Dan shifted his attention from dental work to spiritual work—with himself. He's creating new and deeper relationships with "people who are committed to waking up and improving themselves."

He now works a "comfortable two to three days a week" in his repacked role as holistic orthodontist. He has become a serious student of body/mind psychology, and takes inventive new approaches to healing face, jaw, and teeth injuries, and development problems. He says, "People come to me to consult them and I'll always stop to talk. They can't believe the time I spend with them. By keeping my needs to a minimum, I have the time to 'be present' with my patients at a deeper level."

Dan's office adjacent to his home overlooking the Pacific ocean is a sane oasis for his clients. The office itself reflects Dan's sense of place and his natural way of helping people to heal themselves. The small, simple natural wood setting that looks out through verdant grounds to the ocean rolling in, offers a sharp contrast to the stark lights and machinery that keeps most dental patients away from treatment as long as possible.

Dan's clients visibly change while listening to the ocean and being listened to by Dan. He is an artist at working and his work of art is his emerging holistic practice combined with his ever-deepening sense of place.

## Where Will You Live?

Our vision of the good life dictates "where" we live, and "how" we live. We not only buy a home, we also buy the total environment—neighbors, community services, climate, taxes, and politics. All these interact with our values and influence whether or not our home is an inspiring nutritious place that allows us to express the fullness of our being. For all these reasons and more, it's expedient to give very serious thought to where we will live.

We invent and reinvent ourselves again and again during a lifetime. Changing place can be a big part of that by providing a new outlook in more ways than one. Helen Nearing, in *Loving and Leaving the Good Life*, writes, "When one door closes, another opens . . . into another room, another space, other happenings. There are many doors to open and close in our lives. Some we leave ajar, where we hope and plan to return. Some doors are slammed shut decisively—'No more of that!' Some are closed regretfully, softly—'It was good, but it is over.' Departures entail arrivals somewhere else. Closing a door means opening onto new vistas and ventures, new possibilities, new incentives."

How about you? Are you ready to close a door? Or are you happy and comfortable where you live now? What are you willing to give up for new vistas, ventures, and views?

If you're considering a new place, it's wise to examine what sort of ideal future lifestyle you have in mind, and compare your thoughts with those of your intimates before you go much further. Otherwise, after moving to a new place, people frequently discover that they haven't really wound up with what they wanted, after all. The purpose of this exercise is to help you develop some benchmarks.

## Where Will You Live Exercise

To find out how well your current or future place fits your current desires, rate each factor by number from 1 to 7, with 7 being best. Consider two different places. Place A is where you are now. For place B, consider places you dream of living. Consider places you discovered or learned about through work, vacations, or areas that intrigue you because of your special interests. In each category, write a score from 1 to 7 based on how well it fits your vision of the good life. (A score of 1 means no fit; 7 is a perfect fit.) A second group of columns is provided for your Dialogue Partner's score. Have them fill out that column and then discuss your results afterwards. Or, to make it even more interesting, photocopy the scale and give the copy to your partner. Each of you should complete both groups of columns. The discussion afterwards promises to be twice as interesting.

## Key Place Characteristics of the Good Life

| | Your Current Place | Your Place B | Partner's Current Place | Partner's Place B |
|---|---|---|---|---|
| **Climate**: Seasons, days of sunshine vs. rainfall, temperature, air quality, etc. | | | | |
| **Environment:** Proximity to mountains, hills, lakes, desert, ocean, rivers, open space, trees, wildlife, cityscape, etc. | | | | |
| **Real Estate:** Architectural styles, choices available, quality, cost/value, commercial property available. | | | | |
| **Medical Services:** Quality of care available in the area, preventative and special needs. | | | | |
| **Transportation:** Commuter stress level, public transportation available, easy air travel, etc. | | | | |
| **Cost of Living:** Expenses, tax rates, cost of "quality of living." | | | | |
| **Culture:** Variety of things to do, retail choices, ethnic diversity, cultural opportunities, etc. | | | | |
| **Community:** Pace of life, congeniality, character of the community, sense of belonging, population density, relatives, etc. | | | | |
| **Personal Safety:** Civic responsibility, public services, crime rate, feeling of safety, etc. | | | | |
| **Education:** Public/private schools, colleges and university access, lifelong learning activities available, etc. | | | | |
| **Religion and Politics:** Religious and racial tolerance, diversity of religious experience available, political climate, etc. | | | | |
| **Recreation and Leisure:** Sports (amateur and pro), recreational facilities, night life, restaurants, hobbies, special interests, etc. | | | | |
| **Work Alternatives:** Job market, opportunities for advancement and/or career change, local economy, business services, etc. | | | | |
| **Family and/or Partner Opportunities:** Opportunities for your family, spouse or partner to take part in what the community has to offer, etc. | | | | |
| **Totals:** | | | | |

## Scoring

| | |
|---|---|
| 80 and above: | This place fits your definition of the good life. Enjoy your good fortune! (Or think about packing up and moving there.) |
| 65 to 79: | There are parts of the good life missing from this place. Explore ways to make this place more livable. |
| 50 to 64: | This is an okay place to live based on your vision of the good life. But what's your Plan B? |
| 35 to 50: | This place does not fit your vision of the good life. Decide your timetable and priorities for making changes. |
| under 35: | This place is a really poor fit for your vision of the good life. It looks like it's time to move. Soon. |

Having completed this exercise, answer the following questions with your Dialogue Partner.

- Am I where I want to be?
- Do I know of a place I'd rather be?
- What makes a place "the place" for me?
- How can I make the place I am be more like the place I'd like it to be?
- Should I stay or should I go?

# Look Before You Leave

After all this, if you've decided that you want to move, there are some sound words to be said, based on the experiences of many that have gone the same route before you. It's wiser to "look before you leave" than to leap before looking, for a number of reasons. Here are a few ways for you to sample your future place before actually committing to moving there.

1. *Find someone doing the work that you want to do.*
   This is your key resource. Ask everyone you know or
   come in contact with if they know somebody doing
   your kind of work in this place. Interviews in person
   can give you a "feel for the place" and the critical information you need to make a decision. Your critical question probably is, "Can I earn a sustainable income
   there?" Find out whether your motivated talents have a
   market in the immediate community or nearby. Is there
   a way of checking out the local job market before fully
   committing? Can you apprentice, moonlight, or work
   on vacation time? If you're planning to change fields, or
   start up a new business, begin by talking to experts in
   your field. If you tell the truth about why you want to
   talk to them, the majority will tell you what you want
   to know. Be open and honest about your intentions,
   even if you pose a competitive threat to your
   interviewer. The key question to ask yourself is, "What
   value can I add to this place?"

2. *Write to the local Chamber of Commerce for referrals.*
   Tell them the key ingredients of the place you're interested in finding out about. Seek their advice about
   whether the community provides what you're looking
   for.

3. *Subscribe to the local newspaper in the place that
   interests you.*
   You'll get a general feel for the area, because the paper
   talks to and about the locals. Could you imagine yourself as one of them?

4. *Weekend Getaway.*
   Take a weekend vacation in the place that interests
   you. Relax and enjoy yourself. This doesn't have to be
   "decision weekend." You want to poke around in many

areas of the place. Try out everything—restaurants, recreation, learning. Talk to the locals, ask hundreds of questions.

5. *Take a longer vacation there.*
   Make a second visit. The longer you can stay, the better feeling you'll get for the place. Consider yourself a future asset to the place—someone who has value to add to the community. Look into real estate opportunities. Ask local real estate agents to show you around. Make a list of questions you have about the local housing market. Drive around to get the big picture of what is for sale and what is for rent in the community. Talk with people in neighborhoods and ask them any questions you have in mind.

# Postcard Exercise

## "Where Will You Live?"

Now that you've reflected on "Where Will You Live?," you need to focus on those elements that are most important to you. This exercise will help you figure out which items on your list are most important.

Try to create a mental picture of the place you want to live. The more clearly you can imagine it, the easier it will be to work with.

1. Imagine you are visiting your ideal place—whether it's where you live now or your Plan B. Create an image on the front of the card that represents the key elements of the place.

2. On the back of the postcard, write a note to your Dialogue Partner explaining why you love this place so much.

For example:

"I'm still earning my living as a teacher but only work as a part-time substitute. I've started my own consulting business working with parents and students helping them to decide on appropriate colleges. I have many days to spend with my spouse. We go backpacking at least one weekend a month. We own enough land that we are able to have our dogs and cats in a healthy environment. I exercise regularly because I have such a balanced lifestyle. I have a lot more time and energy to actually read in the evenings without falling asleep on my book."

3. Send the postcard and after your partner receives it, discuss the "Where Will You Live?" exercise together. Test out if you still feel the way you do about the place after you talk with people whose opinions you respect.

# CHAPTER 10

# Where Do You Unpack?

*"Lives based on having are less free than*
*lives based on either doing or being."*
— WILLIAM JAMES

## How's It Going?

Do you have time to answer? Or do you, like many people these days, feel too overwhelmed to even think straight, much less answer straight.

The alarm clock goes off at 5:30 A.M. Three snooze alarms later, you stagger into the shower, already behind schedule. You throw on some clothes, slam down your breakfast, and tear out the door. There's no peace and quiet on the way to the office—if you're not racing through traffic making calls on your cellular phone, your mind is racing ahead to calls you need to make the instant you arrive at work. Errands, deadlines, and meetings press in at you from all sides. Your "to-do" list looks like an airport schedule—only in your case, everything has to be on time. It's said that the average executive never gets more than six consecutive minutes to concentrate on any one issue. To you, that sounds like a real luxury. You've got to juggle at least two things at all times just to keep from falling behind. "Ask me how it's going? I'll tell you! It's going! It's going! It's going!"

When did you last have time to relax, slow down, and fully unpack? And where in the world were you able to do that? When was the last time you asked yourself "how's it going?" And to where did you retreat in order to hear the answer?

Ironically, as we make more and more of our "mark" in the world, less and less of the world is actually ours. As we develop the skills and financial resources that open doors, we pull others closed behind us until the space we have is all but gone. We fill our days so full that we have no room to unpack—even if we did have the time to do so. And even more ironically, the more we need to unpack, the less we're able to.

The quest for the good life is a product of daily schedules and nightly dreams but in order to really live it, you need to find a place beyond schedules and outside of dreams, a place where time seems to stand still and you can stand still within it.

We develop our vision of the good life by talking about it, by shaping it through dialogue and conversation, but in order to truly experience the reality of that vision, we also need to periodically take a vacation from words. We need to stop talking, and listen—listen to what our hearts, our bodies, and the world around us is saying. To do this, we need to find a "listening point" somewhere on the path. Frederic Lehrman, in *The Sacred Landscape*, said that a listening point is "where the earth's voices can be heard more clearly. Go to these places and listen. Once you've heard her, she can reach you anywhere."

Where do you go to let the earth's voices reach you? Where is your listening point?

## Listening Point

Sigurd Olson, in his book, *Listening Point*, writes: "I named this place Listening Point because only when one comes to listen, only when one is aware and still, can things be seen and heard. Everyone has a listening point somewhere."

Where is your listening point? Where are your places of quiet where the universe can be contemplated with awe?

Larrie Christie, a successful insurance agent, leaves for his listening point at noon every Friday. The five hour drive to his log cabin on Tait Lake in northern Minnesota has become a listening point in itself. During the drive, he listens to tapes of poetry and classic literature on his car stereo. Larry says of his cabin, "It's my spiritual refuge where the good life prevails. My wife Jean and I consider it 'home.' We read, journal, listen to classical music, and take long walks with our dog.

I really love my life now at age 60," he says. "I feel like I've spent a lot of time planting, now I'm harvesting. Today, love and place get more of my attention than work. I'm putting less pressure on myself. I know I'll never retire, but I'll downshift soon to working only three days a week so I can spend even more quiet time at the cabin. It's the place that really opens my soul."

One of Dick's listening points is his 110-year-old log cabin on the edge of the Chequamegon National Forest, an area of over a million acres of forest, lakes, and rivers that make up northwestern Wisconsin's "Great Divide" country. Dick comments:

> When I'm up there, my pace, like that of the seasons
> around me, is slow and deliberate. I don't have a telephone
> or even electricity. The evenings are warmed by the
> romantic shadows of the woodstove and kerosene lamps.
> For the past 10 years, I have used this cabin as one of my
> listening points for writing and renewal.

At different times in our lives, we all yearn for a listening point— a place to unpack and be fully ourselves. But few act on that yearning. One who did stop to listen to the sound of a different drummer was Henry Thoreau. He explained his reasons for living alone in the woods by Walden Pond: "I went to the woods because I wished to live deliberately, to front only the essential facts of life, and see if I could not learn what it had to teach, and not, when I came to die, discover that I had not lived."

Dick admits that his motivations are similar:

> There are many times when I finish my writing, don my hiking boots, and walk off into the woods. Times when my walk is interrupted by a deer or black bear shuffling down the path. On these walks, it often strikes me that the most alive people I know all take some time to be quiet. They know how to be present in most situations in which they find themselves because they take time to listen to themselves.

In 1933, Admiral Richard E. Byrd decided to spend the seven dark months of Antarctic winter alone at a weather station deep in the continent's interior. "I wanted to sink roots into some replenishing philosophy," he said. He discovered "the sheer excitement of silence." During that time he wrote, "There were moments when I felt more alive than at any other time in my life." Byrd realized that "half the confusion in the world comes from not knowing how little we need."

Of course, you don't have to seclude yourself away in the Antarctic to hear the sounds of silence.

Dave finds his listening point in the heart of the city:

> On summer nights especially, I like to get on my bike and tool around the city. I feel an incredible sense of freedom in being able to observe life all around me, but at the same time, I'm not trapped in traffic or on crowded sidewalks or in smoky bars. I listen to the sound of the wind rushing around my helmet mingled with snatches of conversations I catch as I ride past. The ongoing collage of images sweeping past my field of vision expands my mind. I get my best creative work done alone in the night air, just me, my bicycle, and those half-million stories in the naked city swirling about.

Management consultant Tom Thiss feels a sense of place reading stirring prose, standing in a historic spot or place of natural beauty, listening to a Beethoven symphony, or discussing a stimulating idea. He says, "I fed my 5-month-old granddaughter alone for the first time and it was the most serene thing. Who could not be softened by that? When I'm fully present in any place today, I expect miracles."

Until recently, Tom, like many of us, derived his sense of the good life from the lifestyle he'd constructed around him. It was a lifestyle with little, if any, room to pause for reflection. It took a real crisis for him to pause and consider whether this was really the place he wanted to be.

"I got so caught up in what I had to do, what others expected of me, that I didn't make my vision my priority. Somewhere along the way, I lost my sense of what I wanted, at heart, to be about. Then, I discovered I had prostate cancer. Suddenly time became irrelevant. The 'quality of moment' became my new definition of the good life.

"You have to align the heart, the head, and the body in the healing process. I wish I'd known that earlier in my life. Because now everything takes on a richness—everything is qualitatively richer. I can be awed by the color of a poinsettia plant. I think you find this presence in children, in simpler folks, or maybe in more primitive societies where life, as Thoreau says, 'is closer to the bone.'"

Tom spends two hours a day now doing yoga, meditating, and reflecting. He says, "It's my highest priority. I organize my daily schedule with care and routinely stop to listen and question whether my intended activities reinforce what I value. I try to make my calendar support my purpose. It's not easy for me to stay on purpose, to listen to my intuitive messages. My routine supports my sense of order and beauty, and ultimately, my sense of place in the universe."

# A Vacation From Words

The average adult American speaks approximately 5000 words a day. And the more successful we become, the more talking we tend to do. Words come spilling out of us, often with great intensity. We have so much to say, there's never time to listen—not to anyone else, and certainly not to ourselves.

That's a why a 24-hour "mini-vacation" from words at your favorite listening point can be so significant. A vacation from words provides a unique way to experience self-renewal. It's an opportunity to unpack everything for a brief period, even in the face of overwhelming "busy-ness." It's a chance to find a new reason—or rediscovering an old one—for getting up in the morning.

A 24-hour retreat to your listening point allows the truth to creep back into your life. It enables you to ask yourself, "What is this situation I'm in, or person I'm involved with, trying to teach me?" And above all, it provides you the space you need to really hear the answer.

Following are ten points you may choose to reflect on in your listening point. Some of these are ideas touched on in other parts of this book. Others are issues we've thought about during our own periods of reflection. In either case, we encourage you to find time at your listening point to take a vacation from words and consider one or more of the items listed here. You don't have to talk about these with anyone—just listen.

## Repacking Reflections

1. *Rediscover your hidden talents.*
   Life at its source is about creating. Talents are the creative core of your life. What are you creating? Are you expressing your talents fully? If not, how can you?

2. *Reclaim your purpose.*
   Talents develop best in the crucible of purpose. When

you're using your talents in support of something you truly believe in, you feel more energetic, more committed, and more enthusiastic about everything you do. Have you reclaimed your purpose? If not, what can you do to own it?

3. *Reinvent your job.*

   Satisfaction always leads to dissatisfaction. Most things repeated over and over become mechanical. Even the things we love best become stale if we don't renew them regularly. Are you regularly reinventing your job? Are you continually looking for new problems to solve, new issues to be passionate about? How can you reinvent your job so that you get up every morning (or at least most mornings) excited about the prospects ahead?

4. *Reelect your personal board of directors.*

   Most of us can trace our successes to pivotal support from other people. What are the important relationships that have sustained you along the way? Who are the people in your life that you've relied on for counsel and advice? Think of them as your own personal board of directors. Picture yourself at a board meeting with these people. You're all around the table. Who sits at the head? Do you? If you were sitting there right now, what issues would you bring before the board? How would you like them to react, and what kind of support are you looking for?

5. *Resharpen your growth edge.*

   If the rate at which you're learning is not equal to or greater than the rate of change today, you'll soon be obsolete. Just like a successful company, you need to engage in serious research and development. Research new opportunities, and develop new skills. Learning brings aliveness. What are you excited about learning? How can you continually sharpen your growth edge?

6. *Repack your relationship bags.*

   Many of us, even in our deepest, most personal relationships, have a bag by the door partially packed. Consider the primary relationships in your life. Are you and your loved ones having "radical conversations"? Does it feel like you're creating a "grand dialogue"? The number one cause of relationship problems is suppressed communication. How can you fully unpack with your loved ones and open the door for deeper, more meaningful communication?

7. *Reframe your time boundaries.*

   Sit down with your calendar and your checkbook. Review how you're spending two of your most valuable currencies—your time and your money. Are you satisfied with where your time and money are going? When was the last time you went to sleep at night saying, "this was a well-spent day"? Are you consistently saying "no" to the less important things in your life and "yes" to your real priorities?

8. *Rewrite your own vision of the good life.*

   The self-fulfilling prophecy is the surest of all—if you can dream it, you can do it. Beware of waking up sometime in the future and finding out that you've been living someone else's vision of the good life. Look forward. Dream a little. What does success really look like to you? It's December 31st, 11:59 P.M., 1999. The new millennium is dawning. Where are you? Who are you with? What work are you doing? Are you living on purpose?

9. *Renew yourself daily.*

   Are you "always going somewhere, never being anywhere"? Have you succumbed to the "hurry sickness" so common in today's society? If your brain is always filled with the noise and chatter of modern living, then you're exhibiting the symptoms. If your heart and mind feel numb, then you know you've got it. The antidote: regular time outs. Mini vacations. Appointments with yourself. Even fifteen minutes or so a day can work wonders. Have you found a regular time and place to be alone, to renew yourself on a daily basis?

10. *Refind your smile.*

The average person smiles fifteen times a day. Does that seem like a lot or a little to you? Are you having fun yet? Are you experiencing real joy? Fun and joy are different. Fun is an outer expression, joy is an inner glow. Joy is derived from a harmony among place, love, work, and purpose. Are you feeling more or less joy in your life than you did last year at this time? Why or why not?

# Postcard Exercise

## Listening Point

Having spent—or at least thought about spending—time alone in your listening point, it's worthwhile considering who you might include on another visit. Here's a brief postcard exercise to help you do that.

*What is your listening point?*

Imagine that you can travel to any "listening point" in the world for a weekend to consult a wise person about the good life.

1. On the front of the postcard, create or clip an image of the place you would travel to to write and reflect—a place where you can contemplate the big picture of your life.

2. On the back of the postcard, write the major good life question(s) about which you'd like a wise person's counsel.

3. Address the postcard to the person you'd most like counsel from. This person can be known or unknown to you, living or dead, famous or infamous.

4. Send the postcard to a Dialogue Partner and discuss your "listening point" with them. Where is it? How often do you go there? What good life questions do you reflect on and how?

# Repacking Your Bags

# CHAPTER 11

# What Do I Want to Carry?

*"Buddha left a road map, Jesus left a road map,
Krishna left a road map, Rand McNally left a road map.
But you still have to travel the road yourself."*
—STEPHEN LEVINE

## How Little, How Much?

At many points on our journey through life, we have to decide what to take along and what to leave behind. And once we decide, how to carry it.

The decision often centers around the three areas of work, relationships, and place, about which we've been talking. How much work? How many relationships? How many possessions and ties to our place?

Carrying too much weighs us down so heavily with work, people, and possessions that we are exhausted before we reach our destination. Carrying too little leaves us isolated and vulnerable, with little chance of reaching our goals. Our only hope of success is to first take stock of what we need and then figure out what's the best way to carry the load.

So we need to ask ourselves a couple of questions. First, in general, "How much is enough?" And second, in relation to each specific item, "What do I really want to carry?"

We also need to recognize that no matter how well we plan,

our needs will change along the way. Many of the things we lay out on the bed before the trip come to seem a lot less important once we're on the road. It's through experience that we figure out what's really essential and how much we can comfortably carry. As a result, we often need to lighten our load along the way—not just physically, but psychologically as well. With each step up the mountain, we must ask ourselves, "What do we *really* need?"

Dick recalls an experience of doing just that.

I was in Africa, leading a group of twelve trekkers up Mount Kilimanjaro on one of my inventure expeditions. As we labored above the clouds with 50 pound packs, it's not all that surprising that we got around to discussing the "enoughness" questions: What are we carrying? What do we really need?

We wondered aloud about what moments and which situations had given us the most joy. Most of the group settled on the big events—marriages, births of children, promotions, that kind of thing.

But I struggled with the question, turning it over and over in my mind as we continued our ascent. Initially, I considered career highs—writing books, creating programs, giving major speeches—but those didn't quite cut it. Usually, in those situations, I was less happy than I was worried about how they would affect my career, success, or pocketbook.

That evening, while we camped above 15,000 feet, we came up with a new way to frame the question: "When did you last feel truly alive?"

Given that most of us felt half dead from the effects of altitude and exhaustion, it seemed an ironic way to put it. But even more ironic was the blinding glimpse of the obvious I suddenly experienced.

"I know exactly the last time," I blurted. "Now! This is it. I've never felt so alive!"

It wasn't just about climbing the mountain or reaching the summit or having a safari adventure. Being up there together, with no one to help but ourselves, I felt as alive as a soul can feel.

I felt on the edge!

Chasing that feeling of aliveness is what life—and mid-life crises—are all about. It doesn't matter where the aliveness comes from. The feeling can arise from exploring our edges in any number of areas—mind, body, emotions, or spirit.

One of the reasons people get old—lose their aliveness—is that they get weighed down by all their stuff. Richard Gregg called it "voluntary simplicity, the avoidance of exterior clutter, of many possessions irrelevant to the chief purpose of life."

Dave adds his perspective.

I went to college right after high school and dropped out after three weeks. I loaded much too much of what I owned into a knapsack and set out to hitchhike across Canada, from Toronto to Vancouver. The first day out, I sat by the shore of Lake Ontario and wrote in my journal: "For the first time in my life, I'm not afraid of death or anything. I'm doing what I want, and though of course I do not want to die, I could without regrets. I'm living more fully than I ever have."

Now I ask myself how often do I still feel that way?

The answer begins with a simple taking stock, what we call the Repacking Inventory.

## The Repacking Inventory

You do this every day. Inventory is simply asking yourself, "What do I have?" Rushing around the house searching for your car keys is one kind of inventory. Tearing through your closet looking for one last blouse or clean shirt to wear is another.

No matter what form it takes, inventorying is an activity from which we all can learn something. When was the last time you moved? As you packed box after box after box, were you amazed by how much stuff you'd accumulated over the period you'd lived in your house? Did you wish you'd taken the opportunity to do some culling through and winnowing out beforehand?

Dave remembers how his inventory has grown:

> The first time I made a major move in my life (from Pittsburgh to San Francisco after high school), I fit everything I owned into one very large knapsack. Five years later, when moving to Los Angeles, I carried three suitcases on the airplane. Four years after that, when I moved to Santa Fe, New Mexico, my possessions filled up the entire back seat of my Chevy Nova. In Santa Fe, I got married, and when my wife, Jennifer, and I moved to Minnesota a few years later, we required a 12-foot panel truck. The last time we moved, which was after five years here, it took a full-size moving van and three very large young men to transport our worldly goods.

Not all of this accumulation is mindless. But not all is mindful either. The point of your inventory is to simply check out what's there. So we encourage you now to do a quick inventory of your stuff. Take fifteen or twenty minutes to mentally or physically wander through your life. Consider all the things you're carrying. Open all your closets. How much of your accumulation is mindful? And how much is just stuff that's piled up? In other words, how much is helping you get where you're going and how much is just weighing you down?

Most people find this to be an incredibly liberating experience. Our friends Richard and Susie Peterson recently undertook a repacking inventory in which they reassessed everything in their lives—except their deep love and commitment to each other. Everything else could go—place, work, etc.—but the commitment to each other was to stay.

Going through their belongings and separating them into groups to keep, give away, or move to storage, gave them both an amazing new perspective. They quite literally felt a renewed sense of lightness in their lives—a feeling of aliveness that had been buried under the responsibilities associated with all they were carrying.

As you go through your inventory, you may find it useful to separate things into the categories that Richard and Susie used, which follows:

- Things you *can't live without*.
  This is the core foundation category. In Richard and Susie's case, it was their deep and abiding commitment to each other.

- Things you *don't want to live without*.
  These are the things you want to keep. The items that contribute to your appreciation of life, the things you want around you in your home.

- Things you *aren't sure of*.
  These are things you aren't ready to get rid of but which you don't need to have at hand. For Richard and Susie, these are the kind of things that went into storage.

- Things you want to *get rid of*.
  These are items that have outlived their usefulness to you, or which you no longer find beautiful, or which you simply don't want—things that are weighing you down. See how much of a lift you feel by giving them away.

One final note about your inventory. As always, we encourage you to talk about your thinking and conclusions with your Dialogue Partner. Your partner's feedback will be invaluable in helping you make decisions and assessments. And be sure you talk things over with your spouse or partner before you get rid of anything! You never know. Something you want to get rid of could turn out to be someone else's lucky bowling shirt or favorite broken toy.

## How Do You Get To Where You're Going?

There are many ways for people of even modest means to escape the trap of carrying too much, or too much of the wrong thing. All involve making decisions—decisions about what is essential, what really matters. It is possible for harried people to live much as they do now and be much happier. It all boils down to how you answer two questions: "How much is enough?" and "What do I really want to carry?"

In answering these questions, many people make the choice to live a "lifestyle rich in purpose." Indeed, many find that coming to grips with those two questions is the key to improving their quality of life. Answering these two questions is an important step towards bringing your own lifestyle and workstyle into balance. It can also be a ticket to personal fulfillment—to a life that is simpler, less cluttered, yet rich with purpose and meaning.

## Repacking: The Trip Checklist II

We've come now to the part where it's all supposed to happen—Repacking Your Bags. This is it! So now what?

Maybe you feel like Dustin Hoffman as Benjamin in *The Graduate*, who having finally arrived at where he's been heading all his young life, has no idea where he wants to go. His father's business partner exhorts him to get into plastics, but this provides no comfort or direction. The only place Benjamin feels at all consoled is at the bottom of his family's swimming pool, safely secluded in scuba gear and goggles.

Unfortunately, we can't offer you a one word answer like "plastics" to the question of "Now what?" We can, however, remind you that you've done this many times before. Although now you may have a better understanding than ever before of what repacking involves, you should recall that this isn't the first time you've done it.

Any time you've ever moved, gone to a new school, started a different job, fallen in love with another person, even taken a vacation, you've repacked on some level. You've considered the things that matter most to you, thought about how they fit into the life ahead of you, and made decisions accordingly. You've made choices, set some things aside, learned new skills for the journey ahead, and set off. And considering that you're not only here, but still in one piece and reading this, you've obviously done so with some success—even if it's not the level you'd like.

Earlier in this book you used tools like the *Trip Checklist* to help set up for repacking. All this has helped prepare you for the process at hand. The difference is that now you've got a framework for your repacking. A model for where things go and a better idea of how to go about arranging them. We hope that repacking will now feel more like arranging each item in an appropriate and well-designed cutout within a custom-made suitcase.

Lots of times, what really stops people from engaging in a process like this is called "zeteophobia." Zeteophobia is the fear of searching out. It's the feeling that stops so many of us in our tracks—the fear that the decision is just too big to make. We feel that we must decide "now" how we're doing to spend "the rest of our lives"! We see the life/work decisions as being too important—so crucial and overwhelming—that we can't bear to face them. So we avoid repacking until the last possible moment. Or until it's too late.

Too often, when we're faced with decisions like this, their importance paralyzes us. The weight of future possibilities crushes us and we end up entirely unable to make a decision at all. But you can overcome your own zeteophobia by keeping in mind that the decisions you make are not cast in concrete. Remember, repacking is a cradle-to-grave process. It's more than likely that one day in the not too distant future you'll need to repack whatever you are packing today.

## It's Not Earth Shoes

As you get into the process of repacking, you may begin to feel some trepidation about what in the world you've gotten yourself into. Maybe the life you've always wanted isn't actually the life you really want. Maybe things are fine the way they are. Maybe you're not ready for a change.

Well, relax. No matter what you decide, what conclusions you come to, or what decisions you make, "it's not Earth Shoes."

Not Earth Shoes? Back in the 1970's a friend of ours, Chad Worcester, bought a pair of "Earth Shoes." You may remember them. They were soft-sided shoes that featured a recessed heel, which supposedly enabled you to walk more naturally than regular shoes. Perhaps you recall their ads, which featured a footprint in the sand, showing how naturally our heels sink down when we walk.

Earth Shoes weren't the most attractive shoes ever made, but they did have their fifteen minutes of fame. Chad bought himself a pair and wore them out onto the sidewalk. He looked down at his feet and thought how strange his shoes looked. He strolled around a bit and noticed how strange they felt. It struck him that their shape and feel would take some real getting used to. Turning around, he saw a sign in the shoe store advertising Earth Shoes. It read, "Earth Shoes. The *last* pair of shoes you'll *ever* own."

Chad thought the idea was too much to take. He wasn't ready for these to be the last pair of shoes he'd ever own. So he turned right around and traded his Earth Shoes in for a pair of sneakers.

So keep in mind that however you repack, it's not the *last* opportunity you'll ever have to do so. Whatever decision you make, it's not Earth Shoes.

# What You Don't Have to Do

We'd also like to remind you that repacking isn't some mysterious process for which you have no prior experience. Don't forget, you've done this all before.

Repacking may be like exercise, but it isn't the loneliness of the long-distance runner. That's why we encourage you to repack with a Dialogue Partner, or check in regularly as you do so. Putting the process into words with another person allows you to test your theories and ideas before you put them into practice. You're less likely to go off the deep end (not always a mistake, but not always the right thing to do, either) if you talk things over with someone else first.

In order to repack, you *don't* have to:

- Undertake the process all by yourself without help or support from anyone.
- Climb to a mountaintop and commune with the One-ness of everything.
- Sell all your worldly possessions and start over from scratch.
- Quit your job.
- Join the Peace Corps.
- Move from where you're living.
- Get a divorce or get married.
- Solve all the world's problems. (Or even all of your own.)
- Finish the entire process in a single sitting.
- Be afraid to change any conclusions at which you arrive.
- Be afraid to change.

# Some Sample Repackings

There are as many ways to repack as there are people. As you get involved in the process, you'll discover what works and what doesn't for you, and repack accordingly. To help you do that and help you see that your own experience, no matter how unusual, is no stranger than anyone else's, we've included a few sample repackings. Take what you can from these and apply them to your own experience, if possible. Or just take them as proof that if other people can do this, so can you.

### Dave's Repacking

In the spring of 1991, I had an epiphany. On a lark (or perhaps it was the first robin of an incipient mid-life crisis), I had decided to take an *Introduction to Philosophy* course at the University of Minnesota. This was my first exposure to "real" academia since my undergraduate career careened off course in the late 1970s. It was a lovely April evening, but I was trapped inside a small classroom, far off in the corner of an aging hall on the Twin Cities' campus. Around me, my classmates, all younger than me by ten to fifteen years, slumped in their chairs or stared unblinkingly out the window as if by sheer will, they could keep the sun from setting for two more hours until class would be over, thereby preserving time for rollerblading or skateboarding. In the front of the room, my instructor, a grad student, explicated the finer points of David Hume's teleological argument in *Dialogues Concerning Natural Religion.*

Suddenly it occurred to me that I had come home.

As we have said, the word "vocation" comes from the Latin *vocare*, a summoning, a calling; my instructor's voice was summoning me back home, to my true vocation, to my original calling—the study of philosophy.

And so began a repacking that has included resuming my 20-year mission to seek out and find an undergraduate degree. I can't say that the studies have always been easy, or even all that intriguing. Balancing the demands of a freelance business with the need to read esoteric philosophical texts hasn't always been a barrel of laughs. But it's been what I've needed to do. I took off a term when things got too intense, and I found that I didn't feel whole. I felt like I was off track from where I was headed—not that I've always been clear about where that place is.

What I have discovered, though, and what this book in no small way represents is that I'm finally becoming the person I've always been. For most of my life, I was trying to be someone. In the last few years, I've finally learned that the real art is in letting myself reveal to the world the person I am.

The repacking I've engaged in over the last few years has involved several choices:

- Devoting less time to jobs for which I get paid in order to allow myself time to do the work I need to for my own mental and emotional well being.
- Making do with fewer "things" in order to have the experiences—educational and otherwise—that I want.
- Learning to say "no" to other people in order to say "yes" to myself.
- Deepening the existing relationships in my life, as opposed to widening my circle of new relationships.
- Finding beauty and satisfaction within rather than always looking for the next best thing that's out there.
- Taking the long view, learning patience.

I've come to see the repacking experience I've gone through, and continue to go through, as a kind of blessing. And I've tried to express my gratitude for this blessing through my day-to-day activities in the world, including, of course, writing this book with Dick. Three themes of gratitude have emerged:

- Honor the gift
- Receive the present
- Share the fortune

By honor the gift I mean that I want to celebrate—with the full expression of their potential—the unique gifts and talents that I have been born with. By receive the present, I mean I intend to be open to new possibilities and embrace those that come to me. By share the fortune, I mean simply that I feel a solemn responsibility to give back, to offer to others my contribution to our shared humanity. I believe that the current path I've begun offers me the best—in fact, the only—opportunity to manifest these principles, the only real way to hear my true calling.

And who says you can't ever go home?

### Terry Hanford

Several years ago, a physician friend of ours, Dr. Terry Hanford, gave up his Minneapolis-based practice to move with his wife to Romania to open a medical clinic. For him, despite countless logistical problems, the move has been entirely the right one. He loves Romania and the Romanian people. He's with his wife and is fulfilling a lifelong dream by working closely with her. And he's doing the work that for him is the right work—even though it pays a mere fraction of what he was earning in this country.

Terry underwent a significant repacking—far more significant than most of us ever want to or need to do. It wasn't easy, and it took him more than five years to arrange everything. He waited until both of his children were in college. He helped them set up their finances to pay for their educations. He set up a partnership with another physician to slowly but surely take over his practice. Working with his church, Terry made the right connections abroad. He labored over the difficult bureaucracies involved in getting the necessary permits. For the last year before he moved, he shuttled back and forth between the U.S. and Romania as often as twice a month.

There were times when Terry almost gave it up. He seriously considered chucking the idea and retiring to Mexico instead. But his vision of what the good life meant carried him through. Finally, he was able to acquire a building in Romania and begin setting up the clinic. As he established stronger bonds in that country, he steadily let go of his connections here in the U.S.

Finally, his half-decade of work paid off and he and his wife moved overseas.

For Terry, repacking was a struggle, but because he satisfied all four components of what for him constitutes the good life, everything worked out. And it can for you as well.

## Using Trip Checklist II to Repack

Earlier, you were introduced to the *Trip Checklist* as a tool for helping you to decide what really matters and what doesn't. Here it's reproduced as a way to help you assess your repacking.

The items on the *Trip Checklist* are still those necessary for a successful and fulfilling journey ahead. However, as you engage in repacking, the particular form of an item may change. For example, before repacking you may have felt that you were lacking in "Traveler's Checks." After repacking, that number of traveler's checks may seem like plenty. On the other hand, before repacking, you may have felt that you had the "Passport" item covered. Then, after repacking, decided that same degree of purpose may feel like it's insufficient to get you where you want to go. In any case, the *Trip Checklist* can help you decide what you currently have and what you currently need for the journey ahead.

We encourage you to take this opportunity to work with a Dialogue Partner and complete the *Trip Checklist*. Try to identify what form each item takes and whether it's changed from your earlier checklist. Consider the relative importance of each item at this point compared to where you were earlier. Ask yourself about each the question that Koyie asked Dick: *"Does this make you happy?"* If so, are you comfortable with the repacking you've done? If not, what changes can you make?

Keep in mind the two questions that motivate the process: "How much is enough?" and "What do I really want to carry?"

And don't forget, no matter what you decide, it's still not Earth Shoes.

# The Trip Checklist II: 12 Essentials for Repacking

| Checklist Item | Have It | Need It |
|---|:---:|:---:|
| **Passport** | ☐ | ☐ |
| Sense of Purpose—a reason for the trip. | | |
| **Adventuring Spirit** | ☐ | ☐ |
| Willingness to let my spirit roam, to plan my own itinerary. | | |
| **Map** | ☐ | ☐ |
| Sense of direction to my journey. | | |
| **Tickets** | ☐ | ☐ |
| Talents or credentials to explore new places and opportunities. | | |
| **Traveler's Checks** | ☐ | ☐ |
| Enough money to enjoy the trip. | | |
| **Travel Partners** | ☐ | ☐ |
| People to share the experience with. | | |
| **Travel Guides** | ☐ | ☐ |
| Key sources for advice along the way. | | |
| **Luggage** | ☐ | ☐ |
| Appropriate style and size of bags for the trip I am on. | | |
| **Carry-on Bag** | ☐ | ☐ |
| Stuff I need at hand to make the trip enjoyable— books, learning tools, and a sense of humor. | | |
| **Toilet Kit** | ☐ | ☐ |
| Energy and vitality to enjoy the trip. | | |
| **Travel Journal** | ☐ | ☐ |
| Travel tips and key "lessons learned" from past trips. | | |
| **Address Book** | ☐ | ☐ |
| Contacts with important people in my life. | | |

# Repacking Debugging

Regardless of your feelings toward computers (and computer programmers), there is something to be said for the way software tends to be designed. Rather than insisting that everything in a program be perfect the first time, most software engineers write code and then debug it. They know that the first time they put together their program it's not going to be right anyway, so rather than agonizing over every detail, they try to get a version complete so they can look it over and make modifications.

Similarly, it is said that "writing is rewriting." The process of writing a book involves plenty of changes. Usually, the first draft of something is a far cry from where it ends up. This book, for example, went through dozens of rewrites. Over the course of the two years that we worked on it, it became our hobby to get together and reorganize our outline and table of contents. (Who says writers don't know how to have fun!)

The point is, why should life be any different? Why should you have to get your repacking right the first time? Why should you make decisions without trying them out to see if they work and revising them if they don't.

The answer is, *you shouldn't!*

In earlier chapters, we discussed ways to test a place or a work or a love before diving into them. We encourage you to apply those same principles here.

Having repacked, how does it feel? Do your new choices suit you? Are they moving you in the direction you want to go?

In the next chapter, *How Do I Balance the Load?*, we'll look at ways to do your debugging in some depth. Right now, we say:

- Try it out.
- See how it feels.
- Make revisions.
- Repeat as often as necessary.

And when you're ready to move on, do so.

# Postcard Exercise

## Trip Checklist "Need IT"

Having completed the Trip Checklist II, you may find the following postcard exercise useful.

1. Review your Trip Checklist II. Are you quite confident you have all twelve items? Or is there one or more you still need?

2. Pick the one that you still feel most in need of. On the front of the postcard, create an image of it.

3. On the back of the postcard, describe why you need the item and *exactly* how much of it you need. Be precise. For example, if it's "Traveler's Checks," describe precisely how much money you need, in what amount of time, and by when.

4. Send the postcard to your Dialogue Partner. Get together to talk about strategies to get exactly what you need for the journey ahead.

# CHAPTER 12

# How Do I Balance the Load?

*"The ultimate of being successful is the luxury of giving yourself the time to do what you want to do."*
— LEONTYNE PRICE

## Faster Clock Speeds

In an essay entitled *Feminism, the Body, and the Machine*, Wendell Berry explained why, despite the exhortations of friends and colleagues, he was not going to buy a computer to write faster, easier, and more: "Do I then, want to write faster, easier, more? No. My standards are not speed, ease, and quantity. I have already left behind too much evidence that, writing with a pencil, I have written too fast, too easily, and too much. I would like to be a *better* writer, and for that I need help from other humans, not a machine."

Most of us, especially in the context of the contemporary business world, are apt to see Berry as an incurable technophobe, hopelessly out of step with the times. In today's high-tech marketplace, where the benchmarks for quality *are* faster, easier, and too much; speed, ease-of-use and output rule the day.

But what do we really get by setting these up as our highest standards? Does compressing time really give us more to spend as we like? Does saving effort really provide us with more energy for our own interests? Does maximizing our results really ensure that we'll get all we want?

When it comes to computers, we tend to have no doubt that faster is better. A 386 chip is better than a 286 because it processes data more quickly. A 486 is better yet because it is faster still. When we spend money on computers, we are literally buying time—the faster a machine runs, the more we have to pay.

As the pace of technology accelerates, we rush more and more to keep up with it. A pen or pencil moves no faster than the hand that holds it. Our turbocharged RAM-rich desktop powerhouses crunch more data in a split second than any person can in an entire day. Which of us is the tail here, and whose dog is wagging whom?

Ironically, we talk in computer terms of "clock speeds." We want computer chips with faster and faster clock speeds, oscillating at faster and faster frequencies. Is this a metaphor for our lives these days or what?

The question is—as Wendell Berry asks—is faster really better? And the answer—as we would agree—is not necessarily.

## Dying for Deadlines

Most of us in our working lives are driven by deadlines. Product release dates. Fiscal year ends. Final notices. It's no wonder they call them "deadlines," because as many people feel, it's deadlines that are killing them! Is there any escape? We can't really put our feet down and bring everything to a grinding halt, can we? So what's the alternative?

In Charlie Chaplin's classic, *Modern Times*, the Little Tramp is a worker on an assembly line. His boss keeps speeding the line up, faster and faster, until the Tramp finally snaps, is sucked into the assembly line, and becomes part of the machine itself. Isn't this what happens to many of us? Don't we seem to merge with the very forces that drive us on?

But there is hope. When Chaplin's character goes into the machine, he suddenly enters into an almost pastoral realm. There, inside the wheels and cogs of the assembly line, sweet music plays. The line draws him back out and he begins to dance around the factory floor. He's released from his bondage, lighter than air, free. And if Chaplin's character can find this sense of liberation beneath the time crunch of the modern world, so can we.

It begins with an image—the image of an hourglass. Most of us live our lives as if we're in the top of the hourglass. We're rushing around trying to build our sand castles, but as fast as we do so, the sand runs out. The longer we wait, the less sand we have, every minute that goes by is increasingly precious and pressured.

We can change our mindset, though. We can imagine that we're living in the bottom of the hourglass. This way, each minute that passes is adding to our wealth. To our experience. To our ability to build whatever castles we want.

Thoreau tells a story of an artist in the city of Kouroo who sets out to make the perfect staff. Understanding that into a perfect work, time does not enter, he says to himself, "It shall be perfect in all respects, though I do nothing else in my life." The artist then, in his ongoing quest for perfection, transcends time. By the time he has found the perfect wood for his staff and shaped it perfectly, eons have passed, leaving no mark upon him or his work. As he puts the finishing touches on his perfect staff, he sees that the lapse of time he once experienced was but an illusion. In crafting perfection, he has entered a realm that time cannot touch.

In our own lives, when we let ourselves experience the perfection of the present, we do the same thing. When we're not exhausted by what has happened or worried about what's to come, we enter a realm outside—or more appropriately—inside of time. That's how we know we've found the right pace. We're neither ahead of ourselves nor behind. That's what it means to balance the load.

Balancing the four elements of the good life is how we shift our perspective from the top of the hour glass to the bottom.

Because as it turns out, it's not that most of us don't have enough time, it's that *we don't have enough of the kind of time we want.*

If you know where you want to spend your time—on work, love, place, or purpose—and can allocate it accordingly, you won't feel so trapped. You'll feel less weighed down by the demands of your schedule and more in control of where you are headed.

If you find you don't have enough time, there are basically two things you can do:

- Increase your income to "buy more time"
- Simplify your life to "own more time"

Duane Elgin points out in *Voluntary Simplicity:* "We all know where our lives are unnecessarily complicated. We are all painfully aware of the distractions, clutter, and pretense that weigh upon our lives and make our passage through the world more cumbersome and awkward. To live with simplicity is to unburden our lives—to live more direct, unpretentious, and unencumbered relationships with all aspects of our lives: consuming, working, learning, relating, and so on."

Simplicity is not a static condition that you can possess. It is a process to be lived over and over throughout our lives, and that keeps changing and shifting each time you ask, "How much is enough?"

## No Boredom, No Timeouts

By mid-life, many of us feel trapped. By the time we are in our late thirties or early forties, nearly all of us have become specialists in something—work, parenting, whatever. Because our specialties have consumed and continue to consume our time, the underdeveloped parts of ourselves become more obvious.

Carl Jung pointed out that by the time we are 40 or 50 or so, we are bound to feel that our lives are out of balance, merely because we have overfocused our time and neglected parts of ourselves. Our "undiscovered self" yearns to be discovered.

Some of us feel betrayed by our success. Our private thoughts reveal a conflict between staying on the current road or seeking a "road not taken"—a new life direction. We feel confused and unable to sort things out. We go through our days looking in on our lives, aware that we are living on borrowed time, but unable to take a time-out and make changes.

When we give seminars and speeches, people come up to us with the same issue time and time again. They say things like, "I feel trapped. I'm bored beyond tears with what I do. I don't know how I can continue in my current job, but I can't (or won't for financial reasons) leave." "I've reached a plateau in my career. I need to move on and test undeveloped talents." "I need to realize some of my lifelong dreams—like climbing Mt. Kilimanjaro!" They go on to say, "I wish my job gave me more flexibility. How can I take a time-out?"

We encourage these questioners to be like Walter Mitty, James Thurber's famous "time-outer." The message in *The Secret Life of Walter Mitty* is not so much the humor of Mitty's mental time-outs, but that after each of his adventures, he settles back into his old life—with a renewed sense of energy and perspective.

Many years of listening to people's mid-life stories has convinced us of how deeply people hunger for little time-outs. And how much good it does to take them.

Satisfaction always leads to dissatisfaction; that's human nature, like it or not. It's very difficult to sustain a passion for something you've been involved in for many years—whether that's a job, a relationship, or a community. Success always becomes routine and mechanical; that's how it becomes success in the first place. So you have to reinvent yourself. You have to dream of something new to revitalize the old original feelings of aliveness.

When the surprise goes out of life, the life goes out of life, too. You no longer experience the growth edge that got you up in the morning with a smile. Timeouts, though, are wake-up calls on purpose. They give us that new sense of surprise and mystery about what today will bring.

Dick says it was Richard Bolles, author of the best-selling *What Color Is Your Parachute?*, who first challenged him to question his assumptions about taking time out. In a dinner conversation, Richard confronted the craziness of compressing work into the middle years of our lives. He asked Dick, "Why don't you carve out chunks of your retirement along the way instead of saving it all until the last years of your life?"

Dick decided to take Bolles' advice seriously. Since 1974, he has set a goal and averaged 16 weeks a year off. Portions of that time are for writing and reflecting. Other portions are for traveling to places like Africa.

Dick says:

> If it hadn't been for Africa, I'm not sure I could have stayed all these years in this business. The time out I take there each year gives me a context, a means to connect the separate parts of me into a whole. When I return, I never stop thinking of the images, not for a day. Even when it is not in my conscious mind, I can feel it somewhere. It is always there.

Bolles later went on to propose new ways of restructuring our lifestyles and workstyles in his book, *The Three Boxes of Life and How to Get Out of Them*. He noted that traditionally, life has been viewed as being made up of education, work, and retirement.

Because people tend to live longer these days and, in general, are more affluent than their forebearers, a new lifestyle model is needed. Instead of seeing the "retirement" box as 20-some years of old age tagged onto the end of a 30-year or so long "work" box, we can scrap the three boxes and create a new model that is more flexible and fluid and more in keeping with current realities.

Still, most people find it difficult to muster up the courage to say good-bye and let go of the traditional model. The path from childhood to old age is a still straight line for most of us. The forces of inertia and money keep us moving in one direction, with little room for pausing, regrouping, detouring, or taking time-outs.

# Inspire Before You Expire

Time out. What is it? What purpose does it serve? What power does it bring into your life?

Nearly everyone wants time out. Almost everyone needs it eventually. And we're not talking about just an afternoon off. We're talking about a real time-out—a spiritual time-out in the truest sense. The root of the word spirit means to "breathe life into." We can say, then, that a time-out is the opportunity to step back, take a deep breath, and breathe life into your life. It's an aspiration to inspire before you expire.

Elisabeth Kubler-Ross has stated the case for time-outs as eloquently as anyone: "It is the denial of death that is particularly responsible for people living empty, purposeless lives; for when you live as if you will live forever, it becomes too easy to postpone the things you know that you must do. You live your life in preparation for tomorrow or in remembrance of yesterday, and meanwhile, each today is lost."

America is consumed by time. Growing numbers of people feel tired and overwhelmed. We now live in the United States of Exhaustion. No matter what we do for a living, we share a common fear—that the clock will tick away when we aren't looking, leaving us unfulfilled and with no time left to fulfill ourselves.

What would your life be like if you took a time-out? Would your family and friends support you, or would they tell you stories of others who had deviated from the straight path and ended up penniless and unemployable?

The time-out way of thinking about time involves a major lifestyle shift, one that the world is ripe to accept. People know that there must be a better way, they just can't exactly identify what it is. What's important, though, is that, as a culture, we are beginning to realize that there is not just one, but many paths through time. The more we look at how we live, the more we see that the old time barriers no longer serve us, and can be removed.

# Paths Through Time

There is no one-size-fits-all plan for taking time-outs. Ultimately, you will find your own path through time by unpacking and repacking—clarifying the good life as you go.

Even the business community is beginning to realize that changes are necessary. Corporations are becoming aware that to stay competitive, they need to alter their perception of time and its relationship to productivity and fulfillment. The economic and social implications of a burnt out or unfulfilled work force are profound.

Bowen H. "Buzz" McCoy was the first participant in a six-month long sabbatical program that the investment banking firm of Morgan Stanley adopted. He wrote about his experience in an article for the *Harvard Business Review*, entitled "The Parable of the Sadhu": "After my three months in Nepal, I spent three months as an executive-in-residence at the Stanford Business School and the Center for Ethics and Social Policy at the Graduate Theological Union at Berkeley. These six months away from my job gave me time to assimilate 20 years of business experience. My thoughts turned often to the meaning of the leadership role in any organization."

During his time-out, McCoy discovered that "there is always time," a perspective shared by another well-known time-outer, Lamar Alexander, former president of the University of Tennessee. In his book *Six Months Off: An American Family's Australian Adventure,* he described his six-month hiatus from politics. The book was inspired by his wife when she said, "We've got to get out of here . . . maybe for a long time, not just some vacation, and as far as we can get. We need to get together again as a family, and you need to think about what to do with the rest of your life."

They found a house in Sydney, Australia. The kids enrolled in school and Lamar set about trying to "do nothing." He read books he hadn't read in 20 years, took long walks, contemplated his vision, and in general, broke patterns he'd been following for years.

What did he learn? After two months of close living, he said, "I think we always loved each other, but we learned to like each other more . . . I suppose we'll look back on it ten years from now and remember the crocodiles and the snowy mountains, but the most important thing will be that we were important enough to each other to take the time to do it while we still could."

It doesn't have to be Nepal or Australia; it doesn't have to be six or even two months. It does, however, have to be a "change in the game"—a break-up and break-down of your usual patterns. We think the following few samples give a pretty clear idea of what we mean.

### Sally LeClaire's Time-out

Sally LeClaire gives herself totally to her work. Every day, she comes home exhausted, with telephone calls and computer work still left to do. By the end of the work week, she literally falls into the weekend, desperate for a rest before facing Monday morning.

A compulsive workaholic? No! Sally is a gifted teacher of gifted and talented students. She knows that higher order thinking skills and creative problem-solving talents are essential in today's world, and she's committed to helping each of her students ignite the learning spark. She believes everyone is gifted because everyone has something unique to express—herself included. Still, even for her, time-outs are critical to her ability to stay inspired.

"I'm still very much on a high," said Sally, as she described the six-month sabbatical she took after 22 years of teaching. "I found that I've got more energy and a better perspective on things as a result of the time-out. It helped me develop new competencies that I liked a lot."

Sally took the six months to renew herself and to finish her Master's degree in Experiential Education. To give an experiential component to her own education, she spent a month trekking and doing field observations in Tanzania.

Her master's thesis sums up the benefit of this time-out: "If my life is a heroic quest, a journey during which I discover my purpose, then how can my life be an expression of what matters to me? How can I be a model of my concern for planetary biodiversity? Through my experiences in Africa . . . I have further clarified my personal and professional commitment to confronting the biological diversity crisis." She goes on to say, "I always strive for new learning experiences. I hope there is reincarnation," she adds with a laugh, "because I would try other careers the next time around. I would probably teach for a while . . . then I might settle down and become a naturalist."

Several years ago, Sally took a one year time-out to live in Mount Shasta, California. It was the first time since she was three years old that she didn't go to school every day. She explains, "I had a deep intuitive feeling that I needed a major change. My mother had recently died, and it was a jarring wake-up call to me. I felt so alone, yet so free—like I had an unlimited choice in my life. I was more of a "choice maker," seeing my life through a new filter. In Mount Shasta, I was doing important 'inner business,' and was inspired by the new people that I met. They seemed to be consciously living many of the values I valued. It was a great opportunity to rediscover what I really wanted. And what I really wanted was to come back to my roots.

"My strong sense of place drew me back to Minnesota—particularly the St. Croix River Valley. Like a homing pigeon coming back, I was pulled by instinct. I felt I belonged here."

Unless she had left, she would never have known where home was.

Louis Armstrong defined jazz when he said: "I know it when I hear it, but I can't tell you what it is." In the same way, people like Sally know the need for a time-out when they feel it, even if they can't tell you exactly how they'll do it. A time-out gives them time to clarify their feelings and hear their inner music.

Sally sums it up by saying, "Once you experience time-outs like this, you want to go back and do it again. After each one, I was on an emotional high for weeks. Thinking about this later, I figured that this feeling came from the daily freedom that allowed me an almost constant stimulation of new experiences, new challenges. "

### Valerie Goodwin's Time-out

Dick's brochure for his "Inventure Expeditions" in Africa claims, "Visiting Africa for the first time, most people have little idea of what to expect either of the place or the people. Going home, they know they have been touched by something. Somehow, it just changes your life. Few places on earth can offer wilderness so complete or tranquillity so profound."

Valerie Goodwin celebrated her 44th birthday "inventuring" around a roaring acacia wood campfire in a remote part of Tanzania. Spending a three-week time-out gave Valerie new lessons in "living on the edge" between the known and the unknown. She was reminded that her passion, her fire, her spirit grows keener on the edge, and that it dies down to a mournful ember when she retreats into the safe territory of what is known and approved. She wrote to Dick following her experience: "When you find yourself fitting easily and naturally into a set of conditions, all the places you have never felt at ease are pointed up very clearly. I have struggled for so long with those well-dressed parent meetings, and the children's school, and the business meetings where the successful meet to think and play. But I didn't understand that it was a discomfort of place, and that in another place, I might fit as if I were made for it. I had always thought that it was something in me that was not quite right; it is some relief to think that perhaps it is the setting that is not quite right for me. Not that I can turn my back on the setting for so much of my life, but it no longer has the power to rob me of the secret pleasure and the silent strength that comes from remembering the places where my life shines."

The people you've just read about chose to take a time-out. Other people are forced to take time out for retraining or to start new careers. With millions of people regularly moving in and out of the work force, disengagement and reengagement are becoming authentic survival skills. Professional obsolescence is forcing more people back to school for retooling and retraining. Lifelong learning, in contrast to once-a-life learning, is becoming the norm. Individuals and organizations are trying out all sorts of options— part-time work, part-time retirement, job sharing, hour banks, flex-time, flex-place, retirement rehearsals, flex-year contracts, project-oriented work, telecommuting and sabbaticals. All kinds of time-outs are emerging as real possibilities for more and more people. Some businesses even find it necessary to include time-outs as part of their compensation packages in order to compete for the best and the brightest. Shouldn't you do the same for yourself?

## A Well-Lived Day

At some point, you may choose to take a chunk of your life's time to discover or experience a time-out—new places, new relationships, new work or a new sense or purpose. Perhaps you'll end up "living in the place you belong, with the people you love, doing the right work, on purpose."

As we have talked with people about their time-outs, many have told us that before they took theirs, the idea of doing so seemed impossible. Yet afterwards, emerging with a new life perspective, they wondered why they had waited so long. Sally LeClaire said that each day of her sabbatical felt like a "well-lived day."

How many times do *you* go to bed at night saying, "this was a well-lived day"?

# Postcard Exercise

## Time-Out

During the writing of this book, we have repeatedly been amazed by how many people we have met, particularly mid-life adults, who are openly thinking about, saving for, or taking time-outs. Try to imagine how taking a time-out could affect your life. What would you choose to do for yourself? Take time out right now to write your thoughts down.

1. You've been awarded a three-month sabbatical. The only constraint is that you have to decide in the next 15 minutes how you'll spend the time. If you can't decide, the award will go to another person. On the front of the postcard, create an image of where you'll spend your time (place), with whom you'll spend it (love), and what you'll spend your time doing (work).

2. On the back of the card, jot down the purpose of your sabbatical. Indicate why you feel it ought to be awarded to you.

3. Send your postcard to a Dialogue Partner. Wait for them to respond or if you don't hear from them in about a week or so, call up and see what they think. Discuss the realities of taking a real time-out.

# The
# Freedom
# of the
# Road

# CHAPTER 13

# What If I Get Lost?

*"You must first be on the path, before you
can turn and walk into the wild."*
— GARY SNYDER

## Lost in the Woods

Dave recalls what it feels like to be lost:

> When I was a little boy, my mother's standard response
> when I whined that I had nothing to do was that I should
> "go get lost in the woods." She was kidding, of course,
> and never imagined that her only son might take her sug-
> gestion literally. But one day, I did.
>
> I set out from home about ten in the morning and
> marched straight into the suburban forest that bordered
> our housing development. In less than three hours, I was
> hopelessly lost. I had no idea where home was and no
> sense of direction at all about which way led back.
>
> I ran around in circles, retracing the same pathways
> over and over. I remember passing a particular stand of
> blackberry bushes about six times from half a dozen differ-
> ent directions and feeling like I was doomed to repeat my
> steps for all eternity. Although there was little chance I

might disappear forever in this two or three square miles of well-domesticated woods, it seemed to my seven-year-old brain that this was it. I would never escape. They'd find my bones, gnawed clean of flesh by raccoons and woolly worms.

After another hour or so of frantic searching, I finally found my way into a clearing that led to a hilly pasture. I ran ahead and came face to face with a horse. Terrified and relieved all at once, I burst into tears. My cries attracted the attention of the horse's owner, a kindly older gentleman who owned the hobby farm on which I was now trespassing. He calmed me down, dried my tears, and took me into his house so I could call my mom.

I remember his kitchen perfectly—the dusty light, the smell of baking, the warmth of the hot oven. It had a great big wooden table, just like all farmhouses are supposed to have. His wife, straight from Central Casting's farm-wife department, wore a flowered house dress and gave me freshly-baked cookies as fast as I could eat them.

Of course, by the time my mom showed up, I didn't want to leave. After receiving an invitation from my hosts to come back anytime, though, I agreed to depart. In the car, driving home, Mom asked me why in heaven's name I had found it necessary to take her words at face value and actually go get lost in the woods.

Naturally, I said that I wasn't lost, that I had never been lost, and that my adventure had been planned right from the start. Mom just smiled and kept on driving.

The lesson here is that sometimes, when we're lost, we don't think we are. But also sometimes even when we think we're lost, we're not.

As you repack your bags and set out on the next part of your life's journey, you may often feel lost. If so, it may be worthwhile to take a moment and consider if you really are or if you're just retracing your steps in the forest on your way to somewhere new. On the other hand, it's also valuable to look around if you feel particularly sure of where you are. You may discover that you're deeper in the woods than you think—and that might not be so bad. After all, there's always a chance that cookies are quite close at hand.

## At a Loss About Lost

What does it mean to be lost, anyway? Or how can you be lost when you don't know where you're going? The positive side of this is that if you think you're lost, then you must have some sort of destination in mind.

Let's say you've gone through the repacking process. You've figured out what really matters to you and you've made changes in your life to pack more of what matters into it. But despite all this, you find yourself in a place that doesn't feel right. You don't know why you're here or what you're doing or why you're doing it. You think back to how things were before you made the changes and recall how good you had it. You wonder why you ever listened to the repacking message at all.

But isn't the unknown demon worse than the known demon? Isn't it better to have tried something and failed than to spend the rest of your life wondering how it would have been if you had? Wouldn't you rather end up, as George Bernard Shaw said, "being thoroughly worn out before you are thrown on the scrap heap"?

In our interviews with people in their 60's, 70's, and 80's, a consistent theme has emerged. Most people don't look back on their lives and fear death. The number one fear of these older adults is that their lives have been meaningless—that they haven't lived as fully as possible, taken enough chances, "worn enough purple."

In the movie, *Grumpy Old Men*, Jack Lemmon's 94-year-old

father tells him that the only thing you ever regret in life are the risks you didn't take. If you're lost, at least you've taken the risks, haven't you?

The other positive thing is that if you're lost, at least you know you're lost. But if you think you know exactly where you are and where you're headed, maybe it's just too long since you've stopped to see where you are. You might be lost and not know it.

Feeling lost is the necessary first step in finding yourself. If you're lost, at least you're on your way—even if it doesn't really feel like it.

## Fear of Loss and Loss of Fear

At some level, all fear is fear of the unknown. When we consider repacking and ask ourselves the question, "What if I get lost?" we're really expressing our concerns about the unknown. Concerns like:

- Who will I be if I'm not who I am now?
- Will I still be a lovable human being if I don't do this or have this or drive this?
- Is this really what I want?
- What if I can't find "it"?
- What if I try and fail? Will I get another chance?
- What if I try and succeed? Will I have to repeat my success?

Unfortunately, there's really no way to answer these questions except through experience. In order to overcome our fear of the unknown, we have to get to know it. We have to, in Linda Jadwin's words, "swim in the swamp." Doing so is definitely scary, but it's the only way we'll ever not be scared.

Dave says,

When I was a little boy, I used to lie in my bed at night staring at the closed curtain of my bedroom window terrified by the idea that behind the curtain a leering space alien lay in wait for me. I dared not open it for fear of seeing his terrible green, grizzly, multi-eyed face. So I'd just lie there stock still working myself up into a state of stark terror. Eventually, I became so paralyzed with fear that I couldn't do anything other than whimper softly and hope my parents somehow heard me over their TV set. It wasn't until much later—probably when I was about 14 or so and started leaving my bedroom window open so my friends could sneak in at night or I could sneak out—that it finally occurred to me how I could overcome my fear. I realized that I didn't have to live with it. I could dispel the fear any time it started to grow, just by pulling back the curtain.

Same for repacking. If the idea of it seems terrifying (and there's plenty of reason for it to), the good news is that doing it is the one sure way to make the fear go away. But does knowing this make it any easier? Probably not. It certainly didn't for Albert Brooks' character in his delightfully dark comedy *Lost In America*. In the movie, he and his wife give up their successful middle-class lifestyle to go touring around the country in a Winnebago motor home. They set out on the road, to the music of Steppenwolf's "Born to Be Wild."

But Albert and his wife soon discover that for them, the freedom of the road isn't all it's cracked up to be. And after she loses the family "nest egg" gambling in Las Vegas, they have no choice but to start over from scratch. He gets a job as a school crossing guard and she takes an assistant manager position at a fast food joint. The upshot is that within a few weeks, they've returned to the city and once again working at their old jobs— at a significant reduction in salary. But at least they didn't end up 60 years old, still dreaming about traveling down the wild blue highway, right?

# What To Do If You're Lost

A friend of ours, Sarah Carter, decided to give up her career as a mechanical engineer and return to graduate school to study architecture. Two weeks after enrolling, she knew she'd made a horrible mistake. She missed her home, her job, her friends—everything. Talk about feeling lost. In just two weeks, she'd gone from being a successful businessperson and homeowner to an impoverished college student living in a basement apartment.

Being a skilled outdoorsperson, though, Sarah did what any skilled outdoorsperson does in this kind of situation. She didn't panic. She didn't make any rash moves. She didn't start running around looking for some way out. Instead, she just sat tight. She conserved her energy and regrouped. She remembered to stand still and listen.

Above all, Sarah observed. She observed the situation around her. She considered her reaction to it. She tried to get at the root of her anxiety and find out where it was coming from. She gave herself time to figure out what her options were. What could she change? What couldn't she? What was worth holding on to? What might she just as well give up?

Ultimately, it took Sarah about six months—and several long weekend vacations—to find herself. But find herself she did. She ended up completing her architecture degree and eventually, opening up her own firm. Had she let herself freak out and quit school before she ever really got started, this never would have happened. Instead of feeling—as she does today—that she's found her calling, she'd be feeling more lost than ever in her former life as an engineer.

Of course, the problem for most of us is that we're too impatient. We get too antsy when things aren't perfect. We want our lives to be the way we want them to be now! No waiting, no figuring things out.

So, if you're feeling lost after repacking—or even if you're worried about feeling lost as you consider repacking—the best thing to do is probably nothing. Sit tight. Look around. Feel how you feel. And don't forget to breathe.

## Other Lost Souls

The poet Rumi once wrote: "What have I ever lost by dying?" Rumi's message is that with every time he dies and is reborn, he sees progress. For hundreds of thousands of years, he was a mineral, then for hundreds and thousands more, a plant, then an animal, and finally a human being. You don't have to believe in reincarnation to feel that this makes sense.

Every time you give something up, every time you repack—even if it doesn't work out as planned—there is progress. As long as you keep your eyes, ears, and heart open, there's something to be learned.

Michael Levy, a software engineer we know, shared with us his philosophy of change in regards to romance and work: "You know what the *worst* thing about losing a job or breaking up with a lover is?" he asks. "You always get a *better* one next time!"

That sure seems true to us. Lots of times, people put up with painful situations much longer than they need to. They're afraid to let go because they don't know what's coming next—if anything. But once they're out of them, a whole new world opens up. Freed from the baggage of past patterns, they're able to see a myriad of new possibilities. Their self-worth skyrockets. As a result, they tend to attract more and even better responses, and the process feeds on itself, opening up increasingly richer options all the time.

It's a bittersweet truth, but we see this all the time in older people who have recently lost their spouse. In the period immediately following the death, they feel lost and scared and are apt to spend a lot of time by themselves, hibernating and regrouping. But within a year or so, they have blossomed. You find them taking art classes, doing volunteer work, traveling the world. They look healthier, happier, and more alive than they have in years. For some individuals, the "worst" thing about losing their spouse is that they get a second chance to find themselves.

## Lost (Re)Generation

None of our stories of how people have found themselves when they thought they were lost are intended to make light of what you may be feeling regarding your own repacking adventure. On the contrary, our hope is to let you know you're not alone. Most people, when they go through the repacking process, experience a significant period of adjustment. You don't just radically change your life one day and pick things up right where you left off the next. You need to give yourself time to get used to the changes, to adapt, to get comfortable with what's new and different. You know how it is when you literally repack a bag—things settle to the bottom. It takes a while for the lumps to smooth out and for things to stop rattling around. Same with your life. It takes time for new perspectives and arrangements to feel natural. And there's nothing you can do about this, really. Time is one of those things in life you just can't rush.

In the meantime though, there are lots of things you can do to make the process less painful. Here are a few examples of activities that can help you keep from entirely losing yourself, even if you're feeling kind of lost.

1. *Keep a Journal.* Keeping a daily (or as close to daily as possible) journal of your thoughts, feelings, observations, complaints, etc. is an excellent way to stay in touch with yourself. *What* you actually write isn't so important as *that* you write. The quiet time that you spend journaling (anywhere from 15 minutes on up) provides a place to collect yourself, to remind yourself of who you are and why you've made the repacking choices you've made. It's also a good way to blow off steam. So even if

you don't perceive the benefits of journaling, it's a good bet that your friends and family will.

2. *Take a Field Trip Into Success.* If you're feeling lost, try pretending that you know exactly where you are. Sample the authentic experience of success. If you're having trouble adjusting, try imagining that you've already arrived. Cast yourself into the future—a future in which you're completely repacked and comfortable with all your choices. Take a day or an afternoon to completely set aside all doubts. Decide not to entertain any fears about your future. Test out the mindset of a native of the emotional and physical landscape in which you find yourself. See if some of the doubts you're having don't go away just by ignoring them.

3. *Take a Field Trip Back to Pre-Packing.* If you're really feeling lost, it may be helpful to review what you've left behind. We all have a tendency to remember just the good parts of the past, so it can be useful to revisit it, to recall what wasn't so great. For example, if you've left a job and are feeling nostalgic about it, call up former co-workers and schedule a visit. An hour or so in your old stomping grounds will probably do a pretty good job of reminding you why you're no longer stomping around them.

4. *Have a Friend or Family Member Hold Up A Mirror.* No one says this one will be easy, but it can be pretty effective. The idea here is to have someone you trust feed back to you their impression of your state of affairs. Ask your friend to imagine that he or she is you and that they're describing themselves. Take notes and don't interrupt. See if you don't end up with a better impression of who you are and a clearer idea of how others perceive you.

5. *Focus On One, and Only One Thing.* Often, the reason

we feel lost and overwhelmed is that we're trying to do too much. So it's a good idea to try concentrating on just one thing for while. Instead of trying to juggle all the components of your newly repacked life, focus on just one. Say, for example, your repacking has involved a new job, a new home, new friends and you're trying to get comfortable with all these variables at once. Pick just one and take a few weeks to concentrate solely on it. Don't worry if the others fall by the wayside a little—let them! Once you've gotten this area of your life on more solid footing, you can turn your attention to other areas. But if you try to do everything at once, you may end up never getting anything settled at all.

6. *Pound the Pavement.* We hate to say it, but maybe you're just being lazy. Maybe you feel lost because you haven't tried hard enough to find yourself. Perhaps you haven't talked to as many people as you could have and gotten as much advice as you need. Maybe you haven't put yourself out there for all the available opportunities. You may be experiencing what runners experience just before they "hit the wall." Right now, you're exhausted, but with just a little more effort, you'll break through and feel like you're able to go forever.

7. *Get Outside, Get Inside.* Get "outside" and talk to people. Pick their brains for more information, more tips, more advice, techniques to open doors that have been closed to you. Get "inside" and listen to yourself. Revisit exercises you've done earlier in this book, dialogues you've had with others, conversations you've had with yourself.

8. *Take a Break.* One of the common mistakes of people who are lost is that they keep going around and around in circles. If you feel lost, maybe you're expending more energy than you need to. Maybe you're working too

hard. Instead of using sheer energy to will yourself out of the situation you're in, try instead to flow with the experience. Rather than trying to carry everything along all by yourself, let yourself be carried instead.

## This Too Shall Pass

Like the vaudeville comedian said, "This too shall pass . . . like a kidney stone! Slowly and painfully!"

It's true, though. Nothing—except maybe styrofoam peanuts—lasts forever. No matter how lost you feel, there will come a time when things change. You might, of course, end up feeling even more lost than before. But chances are you'll end up feeling more at home. And with any luck, you'll feel more at home than ever before.

Life is nothing other than a dynamic process. It's impossible to somehow find and catch happiness because as soon as you trap it, it begins to wither. That's actually what repacking is all about—it's a system for helping you with the continuing search. No matter what form that system takes, it has to come from within.

In the 17th century, the philosopher Benedict de Spinoza engaged in his own mid-life repacking. He began by considering the efforts involved in pursuing what most people esteemed as the highest good—riches, fame, and the pleasure of senses. Spinoza concluded that, while these had their attractions, they could never provide him with the authentic happiness for which he was searching. He made a great discovery, which he phrased as follows: "Happiness or unhappiness is made wholly to depend on the quality of the object which we love." If we love fleeting attractions and transitory values, our happiness will be fleeting and transitory as well. On the other hand, if we seek to fix our love to longer-lasting values, our happiness likewise tends to persevere.

Spinoza laid down three principles for how to carry on his life in a manner that would permit him to engage in his ongoing search for what really mattered to him. In summary, these were to:

- Comply with every general custom that does not hinder the attainment of our purpose.

- Indulge ourselves with pleasures only in so far as they are necessary for preserving health.

- Endeavor to obtain sufficient money or other commodities to enable us to preserve our life and health, and to follow such general customs as are consistent with our purpose.

Three hundred or so years later, we're offering pretty much the same advice:

- Figure out what matters and what doesn't.

- Invest your time and energy in the things that do.

- Pack your bags with the things that "enable you to live purposefully" and set aside those that don't.

Which just goes to prove that the more things change, the more they stay the same.

## A Getting Lost Example: "It Doesn't Get Any Better Than This?"

The writing of *Repacking* has been an ongoing dialogue lasting more than two years. During that time, we've had endless discussions, traded countless stories, and swapped innumerable anecdotes. Through our conversations, we've really gotten to know each other. The words and advice we've shared have had an indelible effect on both of our lives. Dave explains that, in regard to his relationship with Dick, this is not an entirely new phenomenon:

> On at least three occasions, Dick has appeared in my life at critical junctures and really made a difference. Interestingly, at all three of those times, things were going

particularly well for me. Leave it to Dick to arrive and totally shake things up.

The first time was in 1987, when I was the head writer for a corporate training company in Santa Fe, New Mexico. Basically, I had it all. I was just married, my job was going great, and I was living on a 10-acre ranch in one of the most beautiful parts of the country, if not the world. Dick came to our company and gave a seminar based on his earlier book, *The Inventurers*. His message was one of self-examination and personal discovery. At that time, I really felt I was living that beer commercial slogan, "It doesn't get any better than this." Dick inspired me to turn that statement into a question. Three months later, I had quit my job, and my wife, Jennifer, and I were on our way to Paris to live the expatriate writer / artist / F. Scott Fitzgerald / Ernest Hemingway dream. The subsequent experience may not have been the stuff of successful advertising campaigns, but it certainly changed my life for the better—even though beforehand, I hadn't thought that was possible.

About three years after that, I was living in Los Angeles, working as an executive for a high-tech company involved in the development of an exciting new multimedia technology. I had come to Minnesota just for fun, at the request of a guy I used to work with. He was trying to recruit me as a writer for a new company he had just joined. I really had no intention of leaving L.A. Things on the coast were fabulous. I was making more money than I ever had before and was becoming an important player in an emerging technology. On my way back home, I ran into Dick, whom I hadn't seen in about a year. We were on the same flight to L.A. Although normally, I hate doing anything other than burying myself in a book while I fly, in this case, I made an exception. Dick and I talked pretty much the entire way across the country. I told him about how well things were going for me and how excited I was by the technological frontiers ahead. Almost off-handedly, I mentioned my offer in Minneapolis and asked him—in light of what I told him about L.A.—what he thought. His response really hit home.

"Do you want to get known for your tools or your talents?" he asked.

Two months later, my wife and I had become Midwesterners. I had made the decision to pursue a track based on my talents—writing—rather than my tools—this new (and by now, obsolete) technology.

The third time Dick forced me to reevaluate my journey was a few years later, when I was with the company I'd left L.A. for. Again, it was a time, when, ostensibly, life could hardly have been better. The corporation I was working for had given my division almost unlimited freedom. In fact, due to a series of reorganizations, we really had no responsibilities. Still, they wanted to keep us employed. The bottom line was that we could do whatever we wanted and still get a paycheck. My colleagues and I played a lot of nerf basketball, had a lot of great lunches, and—when the spirit moved us—even did some pretty good work. Does it get any better than that? I had my doubts.

Dick and I met for a drink one afternoon to get caught up with each other. I told him about my unique situation, fully expecting him to share my glee at how great I was making out. He listened attentively, and then told me a story about his work with the Maasai in Africa and how excited he was to be helping them set up a school. I compared his level of excitement to my own. The struggles he was involved in, and the satisfaction he was deriving from overcoming them bit by bit made my smug complacency seem shallow and meaningless.

The next day, I gave notice at my job and prepared to

go into business for myself. It hasn't always been easy, but it's sure given me a sense of aliveness I never had previously. As a freelancer, I really felt I was using my talents with a certain degree of passion and most of the time with people I cared about in the place (usually my home office) I belonged. Could it get any better than this? Two years ago, I doubted it.

Still, when Dick approached me about collaborating on this project, I probably ought to have been wary. By engaging in conversation with him, was I once again calling into question everything I thought I had—everything that seemed to be as good as it could be?

As it's turned out, it's happened all over again. And my participation in this book is in no small part a testimonial to how the *repacking* process works. Working on it has forced me to apply repacking concepts and questions to my own life. In order to have any integrity whatsoever about what we've written, I've had to deal with these same issues myself—on a personal and emotional level. I've had to have my own mid-life crisis on purpose and repack for my own journey ahead.

What has this entailed? Quite simply, I've had to "walk my talk." I've had to apply the content of this book to my own life. I've had to assess what I've been carrying in terms of work, love, and place.

I found out that—particularly in terms of work—my life was lacking a certain passion. Aside from work on this book (about which I've been incredibly passionate), I really haven't had it. Doing freelance writing for business clients was paying the bills, but it wasn't fulfilling my deeper need to truly give something back to the world—even though I'm not sure what that "something" is.

As I wrote earlier, my repacking has involved rekindling my passion for the study of philosophy. My commitment to that study inspired me to apply to graduate school, and much to my delight (and consternation) I was accepted.

So, as we wind up the final rewrites on this book, I am planning to depart from my life as a full-time freelance writer and embark on a quest to fulfill my lifelong dream of a Ph.D. in Philosophy. Graduate school looms ahead, with all its attendant challenges—particularly for someone who'll be almost two decades older than most of his fellow students.

Am I scared that I'm going to get lost? You bet! But even more frightening was the prospect of passing up this opportunity and always wondering for the rest of my life what might have been.

I have no idea how things are going to play out, what I'm going to do with the degree if I attain it, or even if I'll make it through the first semester. I do know, though, that I'm thrilled by the prospect of change, and passionate about the journey ahead.

Does it get any better than this? I don't know but, as long as I keep having these conversations with Dick, I'm sure I'll find out.

# Postcard Exercise

## Feeling Lost

If you're feeling lost, here's a postcard that might help.

1. Find a quiet place and take a few moments to sit there and collect yourself.

2. Close your eyes and think about your vision of the good life. Consider any obstacles—people, emotions, problems, etc.—that are keeping you from getting where you want to be. Pick which obstacle you think is most significant. Draw an image of that obstacle on the front of the postcard.

3. Write down what kind of support you think would be helpful in moving past this obstacle.

4. Send your postcard to a Dialogue Partner who can provide support for overcoming the obstacle. Wait for them to respond, or if you don't hear from them in about a week or so, call up and see what they think.

# CHAPTER 14

# What If I Don't Get Lost?

*"I'd rather learn from one bird how to sing, than
teach ten thousand stars how to dance."*

—e.e. cummings

## Two American Dreams

There are two American dreams and they seem diametrically
opposed to each other. The first is about freedom, liberty, and the
lure of the new frontier. The second is about safety, security, and
a home in the suburbs. The first is the dream of Jack Kerouac and
Amelia Earhart. The second is the dream of Frank Capra and
Donna Reed.

Both versions of the dream have powerful appeal. Both are
deeply ingrained in our national psyche. Together, both are the
cake we want to have and eat it too.

Most of us constantly go back and forth between them. One
moment, all we want is the sky over our heads and a quiet place
for shelter. The next, we feel we've got to be looking at that sky
through the sunroof of a brand-new private limousine. We're told
by millions of advertisements for thousands of products that we
*can* have it all. But the fact is, most of us don't even know what
*it* is!

This is why so few people—even the most successful among

us—label themselves a success. If you were to interview guests on *The Lifestyles of the Rich and Famous*, you'd find that for a large percentage of them, success is something far off in their future. Most are still yearning and searching for it.

Ever hear of a group called the "Doughnuts"? It is made up of children of extremely successful parents, kids who have been given every advantage, who have always "had it all." They call themselves the "Doughnuts" because they all have lots of "dough," but they're all totally "nuts." The outward signs of success don't make up for failure they feel inside. The center of the "Doughnut" is empty.

For years, we've been asking people to define the good life. No matter what their income, most say that if they only had twice as much as they currently have, they'd be set. They'd have fulfilled the promise of the Declaration of Independence—life, liberty, and the pursuit of happiness. But when they achieve that new level, they're still not fulfilled. It turns out they'd been pursuing *unhappiness* all along.

Ultimately, it all comes back down to a question of how to define the good life. What is it for you? *Freedom or Security?*

In Isak Dinesen's classic, *Out of Africa*, Karen Blixen and Denys Finch-Hatten have a conversation that brings out the tension between freedom and security, between the desire to settle down and be married and the desire for the freedom of the road.

Karen confronts Denys with her knowledge that when he goes away, he doesn't always go on safari. He admits this is true, but insists that it's not meant to hurt her. She responds that nevertheless, it still does hurt, to which he replies: "Karen, I'm with you because I choose to be with you. I don't want to live someone else's idea of how to live. Don't ask me to do that. I don't want to find out one day that I'm at the end of someone else's life. I'm willing to pay for mine, to be lonely sometimes, to die alone if I have to. I think that's fair."

Karen answers that it isn't fair at all. Because by his actions, he's asking her to pay as well.

And this, of course, is much of the struggle when it comes to resolving questions of freedom and security. None of us lives in a vacuum. Our actions and attitudes are completely interconnected with actions and attitudes of others. Unlike Denys Finch-Hatten, the option to simply go away—whether on safari or not—does not openly present itself. Yet at the same time, Finch-Hatten characterizes what many of us yearn for in our lives. We're looking for a way to ensure that we don't end up living someone else's life. We're looking for new frontiers, new adventures, new places where—at least for a little while—we can feel lost.

## Life: The Final Frontier

Star Trek has it all wrong—it's not *space* that's the final frontier. It's *life*. Albert Schweitzer wrote, "Every start upon an untrodden path is a venture which only in unusual circumstances looks sensible and likely to succeed."

Frontiers are the places we can get lost, the places we haven't yet boxed in with fences or straight roads. They are the places that once were a continent wide. Or even wider—as wide as our imaginations. Frontiers symbolize not just new *places*, but also the full *experience* of those places. One of the real pleasures of traveling down untrodden paths is the sense of freedom and independence such travel provides. Ever notice how more outgoing you are when you're in a new town that you know you'll never live in? Because nobody knows you, you can be whomever you want—or whomever you really are.

As humans, we're natural problem solvers. We require new challenges to sustain us. The benefits of frontiers therefore, are not only symbolic, but practical, too. They provide sustenance to our beings *and* our bodies—nourishment in our search for wholeness and for holiness.

Like Denys Finch-Hatten, our friend, Richard "Rocky" Kimball, feels that a safari is not just a safari, but a spiritual and moral quest—a holy necessity. As Rocky puts it, "When our lives are at stake, we form bonds that we have at no other time. On a wilderness trek, everything is simpler, cleaner, more profound."

Rocky explains why he and Dick jumped at the chance to explore new frontiers on a safari into the center of Tanzania: "Neither of us could stay off the open roads for long. I guess we both like dust! Out there, learning is more real than in the hotel conference rooms where we often teach seminars together."

It's like Wendell Berry says: "Solutions have perhaps the most furtive habits of any creatures; they reveal themselves very hesitantly in artificial light, and never enter air-conditioned rooms."

## Back to the Rhythm

Here is Dick's story about how he, Rocky, and their friend and owner of Dorobo Safaris, David Peterson, found a few of those furtive solutions out in the frontier:

"That's it." David Peterson points out ahead to Rocky and me. "The Yaida Valley. Where the Hadzas are."

For several years, David has been talking about going "back to the rhythm"—to travel with the Hadzas and learn their traditional hunter-gatherer ways.

He says he's long been attracted to this wild country, an area which on the map, "has yet to be divided into straight lines." And he's right. Less than half a mile from the road, the last signs of civilization end quite abruptly, and Africa—the real Africa—begins. That means endless thornbush, rough tracks, and in this case, a steep descent into the Yaida Valley. *And an even steeper descent back to the rhythm.*

As we make our way off the edge of a changing world, into a rugged, prehistoric-looking landscape, we literally feel as if we are dropping back into the past.

The earliest inhabitants of Tanzania were hunter-gatherers, who occupied the area some 3,000 to 5,000 years ago. Some of their shelters, stone tools, and weapons have survived. So have the Hadza, who are thought to be remnants of those early people.

"Where's the coke bottle?" Rocky has whispered to me the exact same words that were going through my head. This place, and the people we are meeting, all look like they are straight out of the film, *The Gods Must Be Crazy.*

Our three Hadza guides are wearing cloth that matches the color of the parched ground on which they stand. Each carries a bow about the same size as he is, and each speaks with an intensity that seems at least as dangerous as the poison arrows in his quiver.

Perhaps because of their relative isolation and resistance to outsiders, the Hadza have developed a substantial degree of self-consciousness. As shy as they are, however, they seem genuinely pleased to welcome us to their village and to show us the old ways of hunting and gathering.

In a blinding glimpse of the obvious, I realize that this is not going to be your typical vacation. A vacation, according to the dictionary, is a "respite *from* something." This, on the other hand, is a journey *into* something—what Rocky calls "The Land of I Don't Know." It's a rare opportunity to venture down untrodden paths, to get out from under the safety net of interpreted experience. It's an opportunity that I've really been hungering for.

Rocky says that when he crosses from the "Land of I Know" into the "Land of I Don't Know" that he has to attain a beginner's mind, to be non-judgmental, and to go into situations admitting that he knows nothing at all. He tries to see the people around him as neither strange nor foreign, but simply as people—his own people.

It takes us no more than an hour to cross completely into "The Land of I Don't Know" and to get back to the rhythm I was seeking—where schedules are forgotten and experience feels pure.

We follow behind the Hadza guides as they move silently through the bush, vanishing and then, like apparitions, suddenly reappearing. To see them stalking is a revelation. Here are the original hunter-gatherers, completely in tune with their natural environment. So light are their movements that a dry twig rarely cracks under their feet. Thorns hardly delay them, and when Rocky, David, and I become hopelessly entangled in these "wait-a-bit" bushes, our guides remove them with swift gentleness before the barbs can hook us deeply.

Suddenly, the smallest man, Maroba, stops and fixates on a huge Baobob tree twenty yards away. We hear the whistle of a birdsong, and Maroba whistles back. He points to a small gray bird, about the size of a robin, fluttering from branch to branch.

"He wants to show us the honey, the sweet honey which we like so much," says Maroba. "He is the Honey Guide—a friend of the Hadza."

For the next half hour, we hurry after the bird, as it flies from tree to tree, leading us on. At intervals, it stops and waits, anxious as a dog for its master, whistling for us to hurry. Maroba, his face filled with joy, whistles back.

Finally, the bird alights on a large Acacia tree, to which it directs us with a joyous, anticipatory song. Maroba surveys the tree for a brief moment and quickly locates the beehive in it. He collects a dry clump of grass and sets it on fire by spinning a fire-stick between his hands. Once the fire has taken, he grasps the burning clump and plunges it into a hole in the tree to smoke out the bees.

I'm mesmerized by how he avoids getting stung. Time

and again, he carefully reaches into the hole—all the way up to his shoulder—and pulls out handfuls of honeycomb, wax, and larvae. The first few batches he shovels into his mouth. The rest he shares with his companions and us, leaving an ample portion for the Honey Guide, who, in the tree above, patiently waits his turn.

Throughout the morning, the same scenario repeats itself over and over. New Honey Guides suddenly appear to lead us on other wild treasure hunts. But later, in the growing heat of the African sun, our three Hadza hosts seem to lose their way. One or another of them is constantly zig-zagging away, apparently off to check for landmarks of some sort. I'm amazed that they can find their way back to us, much less out of the bush, and I think that "if *they're* lost, then we're *really* lost, and it's going to take a lot more than a Honey Guide to show us the way home."

To make matters worse, we're all getting pretty thirsty. Nothing like a breakfast of honey and bee larvae to parch the palate. And as far as Rocky, David, and I can tell, this land is as dry as we are. But the Hadza assure us that there is a river nearby that even during the drought will have water.

Just as I'm starting to wish for a "Water Guide" to show up, the Hadza lead us down to the river—several pools of water in the blistering hot sand which appear to have been the watering holes for a herd of zebra the night before. How they found this little oasis is beyond me, but I'm too busy refreshing myself to ask questions.

Rocky, losing steam from heat and the effects of too many helpings of bee pollen and larvae, crashes in the shade of some trees on the river bank. Leaning on his pack in the middle of nowhere, he half-seriously recites one of his favorite poems, "Lost," by David Wagoner:

Stand still. The trees ahead and the bushes beside you
Are not lost. Wherever you are is called Here,
And you must treat it as a powerful stranger,
Must ask permission to know it and be known.
The forest breathes. Listen. It answers,
I have made this place around you.
If you leave it, you may come back again, saying Here.
No two trees are the same to Raven.
No two branches are the same to Wren.
If what a tree or bush does is lost on you,
You are surely lost. Stand still. The forest knows
Where you are. You must let it find you.

## The Secret of Life

In retrospect, Dick realizes that with the Hadza, they were never lost. Which is to say, they always were. But unlike most of us, the Hadza knew how to stand still and listen. To let the trees find them. In their willingness to treat the unknown as a powerful stranger and welcome it into their lives, they demonstrated their understanding of the real secret of life: *The process is everything.*

The Hadza knew how to simultaneously make life happen and let life happen. No matter what they did, they did it with their whole selves—fully present in the moment. Moving joyfully through the harsh environment in a state of flow, they focused on one thing and only one thing at a time. But in doing so, the whole world opened up to them.

Dick recalls what that felt like:

> Never have I traveled with so little, yet never have I felt so secure, so alive! Most of the time, I trek with enough to cover all the contingencies; this time, we just walked off into the bush and started living. At times, I feel that my life has not yet started—that I'm waiting for just the right time to really begin. With the Hadza, I realized that unless, like Maroba, I can learn to see everything as if it

were for the first time, the future will always be a disappointment.

## What's So Bad About Being Lost, Anyway?

When the Hadza "lost" their trail in the forest, they didn't panic. They didn't engage in a lot of frantic activity trying to figure out where they were and where to go next. Instead, they engaged their senses. They listened. They looked. They let themselves experience the experience.

In today's radically changing world, we all feel lost from time to time—or perhaps, most of the time. We keep trying to retrace our steps back to a place that feels familiar, a place to gather our bearings. But those places are gone forever. More than ever before, being lost *is* the familiar place. So we need to find a way, like the Hadza, to turn that experience into a way of finding ourselves.

It takes courage and acceptance—courage to face the new and acceptance of one's need to learn. It's the difference between the attitude of a tourist and an adventurer. The tourist merely visits life, checking sites off a list. The adventurer experiences life, immersing head and heart in the totality of it. Ultimately, the difference has to do with a willingness to get lost.

An entry from Dick's Africa journal the evening after his day with the Hadza makes it clear:

> Being lost in Africa is incredibly important to me. I experience so much about myself—not all of it pleasant—and that's the stuff I need to keep in touch with. This last year, I've spent more time promoting living than I did living. Here today, I realize that I'm tired of trying to promote a sense of hope and living up to others' image of me. Today, I was not explaining life, but living it. And it felt great.
>
> I'm happiest, it seems, out here where life is least

complex. Where life is the simplest, I realize all that matters is love (relationships I have with Andy, Greta, Sally, and those around me), a sense of place (being connected to the earth), and work (doing work that I love). Beyond that, everything is simply maintenance.

> *The Secret of Life*
> We traveled with the Hadza
> We touched our ancient evolving roots
> We went back to the rhythm where nature still leads
> We learned to stand still
> We learned to listen
> We learned to follow the Honey Guide
> We were not lost
> We learned the secret of life:
> *The process is everything.*

## The Process Is Everything

The more people we talk to, the clearer it becomes to us that we're a nation of travelers. Americans average eleven moves in a lifetime. Every year, an estimated 43 million of us—one-fifth of the population—move somewhere new. Given how often we relocate, you might get the impression it's something we look forward to with anticipation and joy. Actually, for most of us, it's just the opposite.

Geographic moves are life's third most stressful event—right after the death of a loved one and divorce. A big part of that stress is because we tend to spend the entire experience out in front of ourselves. We rush along, out of breath, scrambling to reach a new destination where maybe, just maybe, there will be some kind of payoff—maybe the good life we've been chasing.

And yet ironically, most of us would prefer to appreciate the trip. We'd like to experience the journey with our senses open and alive. But for some reason, it usually doesn't work that way. Most people don't enjoy the process—whether it's a move across the country or a move across town. All the effort put into it, isn't worth the payoff. It's too little return for far too much invested.

People who have mastered the art of traveling, though, realize that it isn't about putting in to get something out. It's about an ongoing process where the effort and the payoff are one. Of course the route is going to change along the way and we change with it. We unpack and repack constantly. We have to in order to experience the journey. If we live only for the destination, for some hoped-for success in a far-off future, we're going to totally miss the trip.

Dick admits he knows all about that:

A couple of years ago, I was giving a speech to an insurance industry group in Maui. I noticed a lot of T-shirts in the audience that read, "I Survived the Road to Hana." I asked some people about it and they related tales of how incredibly beautiful it was, with its Seven Sacred Pools, its opportunities for whale-watching, and—of interest to me as a Minnesotan—the grave of Charles Lindbergh there on the tip of Maui.

I had a few hours after my speech before my plane, so after checking a map to assure myself I had time to make it, I pointed my rental car toward Hana and began driving. Thirteen switchbacks into the fifty-four that make up the "road to hell," I pulled over, opened the car door, and threw up.

I not only had not survived the road to Hana, I hadn't even come close! Turning around and heading for the airport, though, I resolved I'd be back.

I told the story of Hana to my 15-year-old daughter, Greta, and she was equally excited by the prospect of visiting there one day. About a year and a half later, the opportunity presented itself. This time it was a vacation in Hawaii with Greta. We added two extra days to the trip so we could include Maui and Hana. All the while over on the plane, we talked about how great it was going to be—the Seven Sacred Pools, the whales, the adventure of surviving the road to Hana.

Finally, the day arrived. We went all out and rented a convertible. With great anticipation, we set off toward our destination. I told Greta we were in for the adventure of our lives, and it wouldn't even take that long. We'd be home in time to spend the afternoon at the beach so she could work on her tan.

At the sixth switchback on the road to Hana, it started raining. We put the convertible top up and discovered the rental car had no air conditioning. This made speed imperative—both to get some airflow going and to get out of the hot, sticky car as quickly as possible.

At the twenty-fifth switchback, Greta implored me to stop. "I'm sick," she cried. "Why are we doing this? I could be at the beach!"

I assured her that she was going to love Hana, that it wasn't much farther, and promised to drive as quickly as possible the last leg of the way. I punched the accelerator as far to the floor as I could.

Finally, we entered Hana—tired, hungry, and cranky. But all we could find to refresh ourselves was an old clapboard Chinese store. We pulled into the parking lot alongside other Hana "survivors," and discovered that there were no restrooms in the vicinity. Greta and I looked at each other in silence. Meanwhile, we overheard the animated conversations of other travelers: "Did you see those whales breaching?" "Yes, but how about those botanical gardens? They were out of this world!" "Definitely, but I've never seen such beautiful trails and vistas!"

After a long moment, Greta broke the tension. "Dad," she said, "I think we missed the trip."

After a brief tour around Hana, which looked pretty much like every other small, beautiful Hawaiian town, we returned slowly, with our convertible top down, back to the beach. The drive was wonderful. We realized that on the road to Hana, it's not Hana that you're going for, it's "the road." It's not the final destination, it's the trip itself.

Greta's statement, "I think we missed the trip," has proved to be a powerful metaphor for describing the way many people live their lives. We use it all the time in speeches, conversations, and seminars—and people seem to know what we're talking about right away. We encourage them—as we encourage you now—to take the rest of the journey more like Dick and Greta did on their return—with the top down. Don't just survive the trip, live it! Enjoy the experience along the way. Remember what the Hadza taught us:

*The process is everything.*

# Must Success Weigh So Much?

*"The wise man travels to discover himself."*
— James Russell Lowell

## Live Passionately for Today and Purposefully for Tomorrow

*"Jambo Dick! Habari gani?"*

Koyie greets me in Swahili, asking for the news. We are standing in the center of his *kraal*, surrounded by about a hundred noisy animals—cows, donkeys, and goats. Koyie looks right at home, but I am shifting around nervously. I feel crowded by the animals and their smell. Even in the cool evening air, it is overpowering.

Koyie's life revolves around his animals. It's understandable because they provide most of what he needs to subsist. Their milk is part of his daily fare; their skin a basic material for clothing; their blood may be used as an emergency ration. Even their dung is used for fuel and building—nothing is wasted.

Koyie and I stand in the semi-darkness discussing cattle. He tells me of the intimate bond that exists between his animals and himself. He knows each of his cattle by voice, by color, and by the names he has for them all.

Two of Koyie's children arrive, lowering their heads for the touch of my hand in greeting. I am deferred to as a *mzee*—an elder—an honor, which I comfort myself, is accorded to persons older than 30.

Koyie leads me toward the *boma* of his first of three wives. Its outer appearance resembles a long oval loaf of brown bread. The curved entrance is a dark tunnel to prevent rain and flies from finding their way into the cool, smoky-smelling living area.

In a small hearth made of three stones, two one-inch sticks are burning to provide a constant light and temperature. On either side are two sleeping coves, neatly crafted with tightly-woven sticks covered by bare skins. One cove is for husband and wife, the other for children or guests.

*"Takwenya."* Koyie's wife, a small woman with large, bright eyes and delicate features, greets me softly in the traditional Maasai man/woman greeting. She continues to breast feed her child while stirring a fresh batch of honey beer.

Honey beer is the traditional Maasai drink for elders and guests at ritual ceremonies. It may take up to three weeks to make. The golden liquid is prepared in a large, round calabash and placed near the fire to ferment under the careful attention of a skilled brewmaster like Koyie's wife.

Standing there, I am struck by the apparent perfection of the scene. It seems to me that here, in this simple *boma*, Koyie has it all—a sense of place, love, meaningful work, and a purpose.

Though his world is small, Koyie's concerns are large. Even now, he is deeply involved in shaping the future of his people and their fight for their own vision of the good life. A true visionary, Koyie can see the coming challenges. The Maasai, like people everywhere, are in the midst of radical change—change where the young are moving ahead of their elders, impatient to discover what the modern world has to offer. So I am doubly impressed by his ability to maintain a sense of quiet calm amidst the building storm.

Offering me a honey beer, Koyie asks, "So Dick, what kind of good life are these people traveling with you seeking? The more people you bring to my village, the clearer it becomes that most are seeking something. At the start of your treks, all these people, all these successful people, seem to be struggling with some heavy weight. So I ask you, *why must success weigh so much?*"

I answer that I think all these people are searching for their own vision of the good life. Then, I ask him what he thinks. He sets down his honey-beer and picks up the new journal and pen that I have brought him as a gift. He writes quickly but neatly in careful strokes. He shows me what he has written, in Maa, the Maasai language: *Meetay oidpa, oitumura ake-etay.*

"It's an old Maasai saying, a definition of the good life," explains Koyie. "It means something like living passionately for today and purposefully for tomorrow. It means you can only enjoy now, no matter how rich you are. It all comes to an end soon."

He keeps trying to make it clearer. "It means being able to be happy today is the real proof of success. It may seem simple to you, Dick, but the good life to me means appreciating all the ways I am already a success—my health, my cattle, children, good rains. What's the use of worrying about enough milk for next week unless I can enjoy the milk now? Does that make sense?"

I sip my honey-beer and reflect on how he has captured

perfectly what I've been striving to say all along. But it's always like this with Koyie. When I'm with him, speaking the language haltingly, feeling like a shy student, I somehow get in touch with and reveal parts of myself that usually remain hidden to others—even to myself. I experience all the basic human vulnerabilities, feelings of incompetence, and deep-seated needs for approval. But somehow, Koyie makes me feel what I think we all know somewhere deep inside—that our true value is more than what we do, how much we make, or how many things we own—it's simply who we are.

"So Dick, what do you think? The best I can offer you and your friends is to live passionately for today and purposefully for tomorrow. Does that help?"

That evening, after I leave Koyie, his words and image remain in my mind, and they hearten me, rekindling my faith in human nature. I see the picture of Koyie, the Maasai elder with his blanket around him, gazing off toward the infinite horizon. Koyie is genuinely living on the edge—on the outer edge of tomorrow, yet at the same time, on the inner edge of today.

*Living passionately for today and purposefully for tomorrow.*

## No Boundaries to Wisdom

Complex change is now the dominant experience of human beings everywhere. The world is pressing in on all of us, no matter where in the world we call home. Individuals, and societies around the globe face the same challenges and questions. We all must adapt to the changes or be swallowed up by them.

The hope in all this is that we will learn from each other. Wisdom from the old and new world can guide our experience and help us move forward together. There are no boundaries to this wisdom, if only we are open to receive it.

Learning to shape and reshape our personal and collective destinies—to pack and repack our bags—is the central lesson of our time. But it is a lesson we all can learn by living passionately for today and purposefully for tomorrow. In doing so, we lighten our loads for the rest of our lives.

# Index

# About the Authors

## *Richard J. Leider*

Richard J. Leider is a  nationally-recognized speaker, author, and trainer in the career development field. As an expert on career and lifestyle strategies for the 21st century, Dick is often quoted in newspapers, magazines, and on radio and television. Dick is the author of three books: *The Inventurers: Excursions in Life and Career Renewal, The Power of Purpose*, and *Life Skills: Taking Charge of Your Personal and Professional Growth*. He has been active with Outward Bound for many years, and his own company, Inventure Expeditions, leads yearly "inventure/adventure" treks in East Africa. Dick has a Master's Degree in Counseling Psychology and is a Nationally Certified Career Counselor. He is founder and partner of *The Inventure Group*, a training consulting firm in Minneapolis, MN.

## *David A. Shapiro*

David A. Shapiro has made a career out of repacking his bags. Having started his professional life by penning jokes for stand-up comedians, David currently specializes in writing programs for businesses and organizations that are interested in helping people to be more than just cogs in the machine. He is also active in the field of interactive multimedia, and is consistently working to discover new ways of merging high-tech with "high-touch" in an effort to assist people in their ongoing life and career development. As of his last repacking, David was living in Seattle, WA. But in these days of extremely portable computers, that may already have changed.